Praise for
Ignite the Third Factor

"If I could have read this book 30 years ago, it would have made me a better leader a lot sooner. It took decades for me to realize that viewing every interaction as an opportunity to help people get better is the key to building a winning enterprise. The funny thing is that, as I read it, I kept thinking how the same principles can be applied to helping your kids develop their potential . . . and there it was . . . in the last chapter!"

> — Gwyn Morgan, Founding CEO, EnCana Corporation

"In his unique and engaging way, Peter has conveyed a wealth of valuable information. I especially liked the final chapter that completed the circle from Olympics, to business, to parenting. I suspect you will love this book as much as I did."

> — Julian Barling, Ph.D., Professor and Associate Dean, Queen's School of Business

". . . fantastic, practical and of great substance! This is not a book of forced parallels between sports and business, but rather a recognition that what 'ignites' greatness in all of us can be found anywhere by a great leader."

> — Shirlee Sharkey, CEO, St. Elizabeth Health Care

"Peter's unique perspective allows him to describe what is truly fundamental to inspiring leadership in a simple, direct and practical way. The book is a pleasure to read – and full of ideas that stay with you long after you put it down."

> — Charlie Fischer, President and CEO, Nexen Inc.

"I have known Peter and watched him work with athletes for 25 years and have seen him use his own grounded self-direction to pull athletes to not only perform but to develop as better people. This book has had a profound impact on me. Well done! He is indeed an *Igniter*." — Brian Williams, CTV Olympic Host

"*Ignite the Third Factor* is a tremendous playbook that explores deeply the key elements that develop people to their greatest potential and brings high performance to the next level. *Ignite the Third Factor* is a great gift for anyone who wants to be the best they can be and develop those around them to do the same."

> — Linda Morgan, Vice President, Human Resources and
> Labour Relations, Reliance Comfort Limited Partnership

"IF YOU DEAL WITH CLIENTS OR SERVICE OPERATIONS, READ THIS BOOK!!! As you read this book, replace the 'athlete/child' with 'customer' and you'll find Jensen's comments could serve as guiding principles for anyone managing customer service or in the business of creating retail experiences. You'll gain innovative insights on how to interact with customers and how to develop meaningful customer relationships. Best of all, while reading how Jensen coaches athletes to elevate their performance, you'll be learning how to get your customers to elevate their level of value from working with you . . . a surefire formula for customer loyalty and long-term success."

> — Ken Wong, Associate Professor, Business and Marketing
> Strategy, Queen's School of Business

"Dr. Peter Jensen has parsed the components of effective leadership with the precision of a track coach preparing elite runners step-by-step for a championship race. Every leader or leader-in-training will benefit from Dr. Jensen's knowledge, research and remarkable insight into the discipline of high-performance leadership."

> — Ian Anderson, Executive Director, Governor General's
> Leadership Conference

IGNITE THE THIRD FACTOR

How Do You Get People Committed to Reaching Their Full Potential?

Dr. Peter Jensen

Thomas Allen Publishers
Toronto

Library and Archives Canada Cataloguing in Publication

Jensen, Peter, 1946–
Ignite the third factor : how do you get people committed
to reaching their full potential? / by Peter Jensen.

Includes bibliographical references.
ISBN 978-0-88762-767-5

1. Employees – Coaching of. 2. Employee motivation.
3. Self-actualization (Psychology). I. Title.

HF5549.5.C53J45   2011   658.3'124   C2010-908134-X

Cover design: Sputnik Design Partners Inc.
Cover image: iStockphoto

Published by Thomas Allen Publishers,
a division of Thomas Allen & Son Limited,
390 Steelcase Road East,
Markham, Ontario L3R 1G2 Canada

www.thomasallen.ca

ONTARIO ARTS COUNCIL
CONSEIL DES ARTS DE L'ONTARIO

Canada Council
for the Arts

The publisher gratefully acknowledges the support of
The Ontario Arts Council for its publishing program.

We acknowledge the support of the Canada Council for the Arts, which last
year invested $20.1 million in writing and publishing throughout Canada.

We acknowledge the Government of Ontario through the Ontario
Media Development Corporation's Ontario Book Initiative.

We acknowledge the financial support of the Government of Canada
through the Canada Book Fund for our publishing activities.

2 3 4 5   16 15 14

Text printed on a 100% PCW recycled stock
Printed and bound in Canada

Dr. Peter Jensen has participated in seven Olympic Games as a member of the Canadian team, worked with over 50 medal-winning athletes and their coaches and was the sport psychology coach for Canada's 2010 Olympic gold medal women's hockey team. He is an instructor at Canada's foremost business school, Queen's School of Business, and the founder of Performance Coaching, a corporate training firm. For more information, please visit: www.peterjensen.ca.

Books of Merit

Acknowledgments

I owe a huge debt of gratitude to all of the coaches I've spent time with and who have allowed me into their world over the past four decades. I am especially indebted to six exceptional Olympic coaches who took the time from their busy schedules to allow me to interview them for this book. Their insight is in the pages that follow.

Mel Davidson, Canadian ice hockey coach
Frank Dick, British decathlon coach and coaching mentor
David Hemery, British Olympic gold medalist and hurdling coach
Andy Higgins, Canadian decathlon coach
Debbie Muir, Canadian and Australian synchronized swimming coach
Gary Winckler, American track and field coach

Figure skating coach Doug Leigh has been a friend for many years and I learned much from him and the skating coaches I worked with at numerous world championships and three Olympic Games.

There is much wisdom in this book from Andy Higgins, with whom I work on a regular basis not only with his athletes but also as a part of a coaching certification program that he coordinates in Toronto.

The late Jack Donahue and the legendary John Wooden had a great influence on me in my brief 10-year stint as a basketball coach. Dr. John Meagher at the University of New Brunswick was a mentor to me and taught me almost everything I know about teaching.

Dr. Kazimierz Dabrowski was in his 70s when he mentored me in graduate school. It was a humbling experience to learn from such a generous human being, one who knew so much more than I could ever imagine knowing. My working with Dr. Dabrowski was a life-altering experience and he, along with Dr. Marlene Rankel, deepened my understanding of human developmental psychology. As you shall see, Dr. Dabrowski's work has had a strong influence on this book.

My wife, Sandra Stark, and I spent a weekend with Marlene, along with Bill and Charmaine Ramer, discussing Dr. Dabrowski's theory and its application here. I am most thankful for that, as I didn't, in any way, want to misrepresent or oversimplify Dr. Dabrowski's most important work.

Sue Rosenthal took on the onerous task of working with me as an editor. She really dove into the project and she not only was good at what she did but also ignited something under me that got it finished on time! She was, as David Hemery put it when referring to one of his coaches, "a hand in the back."

Mebbie Black turned what Sue and I did into much better prose. Her fine touch is everywhere in these pages.

Several people were kind enough to review and comment on the first draft, helping immensely to improve the final product. Thanks to Linda Morgan, Ezra Rosen, Steve Earle, Peggy Baumgartner, Mary Lou Ackerman, Sandra Stark, Shelley Swallow, Mary Ann Pilskalnietas, Barry Rosenthal, Cedric Stevenson, Karyn Garossino and Dane Jensen. And many thanks to Allyson Latta for her terrific job of copy editing.

I work every day with an exceptional team of people at Performance Coaching. Our business manager, Shelley Swallow, and I have been together for more than 20 years. She, with her fine organizational skills, has taken an active role in quarterbacking the publication of this book. Our director of training, Peggy Baumgartner, is the best corporate trainer I have ever seen. She brought her usual energy, enthusiasm and intelligence to the project. Senior associate Garry Watanabe, an ex–Southern California swim coach and former lawyer with a master's in sport psychology (what a combo!), not only was involved in reviewing material for this book but also contributed key examples from his workshop participants.

My son Dane helped me get the idea and concept of the book off the ground, and, along with his brother, James, designed the layout for the website. James also designed the cover for the book. Many thanks also to Robert Ketchen for the design and layout of the book. I owe a huge debt of gratitude to my wife, Sandra, who co-wrote the "When All Else Fails" appendix and who has contributed her wisdom by way of feedback and content.

I dedicate this book to our four grandchildren, Kaili, Madelyn, Aiden, and Brandon; and to those, God willing, that will follow. May they be fortunate enough to have teachers, mentors and bosses who ignite their Third Factor!

— Dr. Peter Jensen
Toronto, August 2008

Contents

Introduction

How did Helen Keller become such an iconic figure in our cultural consciousness? How did Nelson Mandela emerge from a lengthy imprisonment without bitterness, anger and resentment? How did Aleksandr Solzhenitsyn grow up a free thinker in an oppressive culture? There is clearly some factor in the development of certain human beings that transcends culture, upbringing and genetics. Sometimes the influence of another person or persons plays a vital role. Helen Keller, for example, was fortunate to have as her teacher Annie Sullivan, whose part in her development was immense. And Nelson Mandela, in his book *Long Walk to Freedom,* speaks of many people, including writers and historical figures from the past, who strongly influenced who he became.

But there was another factor at work in each of these remarkable individuals—and others whose development has been shaped by more than just genetics and environment. This crucial "Third Factor" is the role individuals choose to play in their own development.

We will soon see that this concept of the Third Factor has very broad application in any arena where pressure and the need for excellence are equally present. For many this is the work world; for others, athletics, academics, or artistic endeavors.

Dr. Kazimierz Dabrowski, a distinguished psychiatrist and my mentor in the 1970s, studied the lives of numerous exceptional human beings and discovered that this Third Factor played a major role in the moral and emotional growth of such individuals.

In my case, working with Olympic athletes and coaches has led to an understanding of the profound power of the Third Factor. Olympic sport provides the ideal "performance laboratory" where the role of the Third Factor can be closely observed. In the world of international athletics, the truly great coaches have a strong developmental bias that is directed at the Third Factor in the performer. Coaches with a strong developmental bias are always concerned with encouraging their performers to engage their Third Factor, to get passionate about developing themselves. Through my 25 years of involvement with the Olympic movement, I have seen first-hand the remarkable outcomes that this produces—both at the Games and afterward, in life.

Kareem Abdul-Jabbar and Bill Walton, former players of legendary basketball coach John Wooden, wax eloquent about him. But it's not about the basketball skills he taught them. It's about the role Coach Wooden played in their development as human beings, encouraging them to be the best they could be and to take an active role in their own growth and development. John Wooden is not unique in this regard. I have worked with many coaches over the years and witnessed their developmental bias and their skill at igniting the Third Factor in their performers. Doug Leigh, one of the world's top figure skating coaches, put it succinctly once when we were discussing a world-class skater late in his career. "In the end," he said, "all you have left is the person."

If you have purchased or are leafing through this book, you already have a fair dose of the Third Factor. People looking for ways to help others improve by getting better at something themselves are engaging their Third Factor in big ways. Similarly, the developmental bias already at work in you may have drawn you to the book's title or contents page.

The Third Factor

The concept of the Third Factor, critical in developing performers, originated with Kazimierz Dabrowski, under whom I studied in 1977 and 1978. I want to make it clear that I am borrowing the concept—which he considered important in the development of moral and emotional growth—and employing it in a much more simplistic manner than he did. I use the term as a way of talking about self-direction and the development of self-awareness and self-responsibility in the people we coach and manage.

Dabrowski believed that developmental potential has three components:

Nature. These factors establish the physical and mental "road map" of the individual. They include genetic as well as other factors such as a mother's alcohol consumption during pregnancy.

Nurture. These are the social and physical (environmental) factors that contribute to the shaping of the individual, such as parents, friends, school, financial status, culture and nationality. "Nurture" modifies your "nature." A good upbringing is obviously an asset, but as we will see, a less-than-ideal upbringing need not limit where you end up. The term *ideal* is also in need of some definition in that a conflict- and adversity-free upbringing sometimes can be limiting in terms of personal growth and development.

The Third Factor. This is the factor of choice. No matter what the genetic and environmental endowments bestowed on individuals, they have the potential to transcend these endowments through the action and power of the Third Factor. The individual can make a conscious choice to *change* and to become a higher-level individual. Simply put, the Third Factor is the important role that an individual plays in his or her own "becoming."

This self-development often happens in times of conflict, when the person becomes dissatisfied in some way with themselves. Initially there may be an external conflict, a failure, loss or disappointment, but the person internalizes it, and the dissatisfaction between "what is" and "what ought to be" is the impetus for the emergence of the Third Factor. We will see that emotion is a critical factor in where performers end up developmentally.

The Third Factor is the key to high performance because it requires engaging the will and becoming increasingly more self-responsible and aware. It's not possible to go back and change or trade in our genetic gifts, or to select "better" parents to re-raise us. What is, is. We have to work with what we have. Nor can people be *pushed* to the highest level. They have to have their own desire to get better at what they're doing. Others, however, most notably leaders, teachers and coaches with developmental bias, *can* take an active role in developing in others the self-sufficiency necessary to perform. And when the developmental bias of a good leader "plugs into" the Third Factor in a performer . . . WOW happens.

Over the past few decades much has been written on self-development, empowerment, personal power and other concepts that, at first blush, would appear to be synonymous with the Third Factor. But much of pop psychology is not about awareness and true self-development. It is more a denial or "riding over" of a person's current reality through conditioning or reprogramming: "Listen to this CD series daily and you'll begin to believe." There are good programs out there, but most are about **pushing** the person to a new place. Igniting the Third Factor is all about **pull**. It is very much grounded in self-direction.

It is not about willpower, a forced changing and driving oneself forward, but more about developing an awareness of free will and our choices. It is about being pulled toward growth. It is not adding a layer of new "to dos," but removing blind spots and seeing what is possible and, again, being pulled by that.

I sometimes think of the Third Factor as an uncovering of what we already possess and a realization of what is therefore possible. It is as if we own an amazing "computer" that has a powerful program of self-development installed, but that remains undiscovered and dormant until the user, often with the help of an exceptional coach, leader or parent, becomes aware of it. Then everything changes and new possibilities arise. In that instant, igniting has occurred, and the Third Factor begins to help the person evolve.

Our understanding of this concept will grow as we progress through the book.

A quick word on terminology. I will use the words *coach, manager* and *leader* interchangeably in what follows. The skills apply to anyone (parent or teacher or coach or manager) developing anyone anywhere. I tend to use the word *coach* more frequently because I believe that is the management style most needed in today's workplace. I want leaders and managers to think of themselves as coaches.

Developmental Bias

Developmental bias is the underpinning for every truly successful coach. Coaches with a developmental bias recognize the importance of, and are passionate about, growing and developing people. Success for these coaches is not only about the results but also about building competence, commitment, capacity and passion in their performers. They take on a bigger role than simply supervising, directing or managing.

Coaches who have a strong developmental bias rarely, if ever, in any way damage those under their care. This is not true of those who serve their own interests from a top-down position. The exceptional coaches stand out because of the results their people are able to produce.

This book is about developing a developmental bias. It is written for anyone with an interest in learning how to help others grow and develop. Some people seem to be born with that urge, but for most of us, a developmental bias emerges gradually, becoming obvious only when we take on a leadership role, and continues to develop through our diligent efforts and under changing circumstances.

In the work world, and indeed also in the sporting world, it is essential to continually learn and get better at whatever it is you're doing. There are many reasons for this, which we will go into later, the most obvious being that the bar is always being raised. We live in a world of endless change, where last year's results will rarely do next year, and certainly not in the years to follow.

The Exceptional Coach as Gardener

My father, Anker Jensen, immigrated to Canada from Denmark in March of 1930, at the beginning of the Great Depression that followed the stock market crash of 1929—not an ideal time for a 20-year-old to try to forge a new life in North America. He came into Canada, as did all immigrants at that time, through Pier 21, the Canadian equivalent of Ellis Island, in Halifax, Nova Scotia. My father died in 1976, and I know very little of his past in Denmark, but a few years ago I spent a day at Pier 21 and managed to trace all his records from that time. In Canada, he worked in a mine in northern Quebec for 42 years and served for five years with the Canadian forces in the Second World War, but interest-ingly—and revealingly—the ship documents on his entry to this coun-try had him listed as a farm laborer.

Despite the climate and the poor soil conditions in Noranda, where I was born and raised, my father always had an amazing garden. Some of the neighbors tried to follow his example, but their gardens were never quite as fruitful as his. There was a reason for this, of course. A natural gardener, my father knew how to create the right conditions to maxi-mize the growth potential that lies dormant in every plant. He spent many hours tending the beds and enriching the clay soil in our backyard with compost from a bin he had built in the back corner. Similarly, good coaches, leaders and parents nourish their charges and thus get a lot more commitment out of them than poor coaches, leaders and parents ever could. And they do it the same way a gardener does: by creating an environment that stimulates growth.

In developing people, the challenge is not about physical growth but about igniting in them the desire to achieve their potential, whatever their focus. When we speak of commitment, it is about commitment to themselves and their own growth and development, rather than to anything outside the person, such as an organization. We want them to begin using all of their talents and skills to become the best they can be. We want them to activate their Third Factor.

Without stimulation and encouragement, a life-altering event, or a nurturing mentor/coach, the Third Factor can go unrealized, just as, in the gardening analogy above, a plant's potential for growth may go un-realized until a gardener with the skill to stimulate it comes along.

Five Characteristics of Exceptional Coaches

My studies of exceptional coaches have revealed five characteristics that enable them to ignite the Third Factor.

- **Self-awareness**, which equips them to assist, not inhibit, the ignit-ing of Third Factor
- **Ability to build trust**, so that the first steps toward gradually attaining self-direction can be taken in a relatively safe and secure environment

- **Ability to use imagery** to help the person "see" what is possible and thus to encourage the process of belief in the self
- **Ability to identify blocks when they occur** and to help the person take responsibility for dealing with these temporary barriers
- **Recognizing the importance of adversity,** which is critical at some point to determine the strength of the person's commitment to themselves and their performance. Learning to embrace adversity and focus on what can be controlled is essential in developing the Third Factor in the performer—a preparation for moving out of the performance laboratory and into the bigger arena of life.

Over years of involvement in the corporate world and the world of Olympic and international sport, it has become obvious to me that a developmental bias is the foundation for effective coaching. The exceptional coaches I've had the good fortune to spend time with have all had an incredibly strong developmental bias. Without exception, they have also been very practical people. This book has the same focus. It's a practical "playbook" that you can use to get much better at developing others.

This book, though written particularly for use in the workplace, is ultimately a practical guide to using coaching as a tool in any realm where the principles and techniques are applicable. You will hear a lot about what exceptional athletic coaches do, but as leaders in the business community you should know that when I talk to athletic coaches, I talk to them about what great business leaders do! When I'm training them, I routinely ask them to review a business leadership book and tell me what they learned from it that they can use on a daily basis. They never fail to discover valuable skills and techniques that help them become better athletic coaches. This book, in a way, turns those tables. You will find here lessons from these exceptional Olympic coaches that will be of value to you in your day-to-day responsibilities as a leader.

Leaders with a strong developmental bias spend a great deal of time playing out various scenarios and imagined consequences. They take leading and developing seriously and are open to new learning. As Coach Wooden puts it, "It's what you learn after you know everything that matters."

For those with a strong developmental bias, the line blurs between work and play, person and profession. Their impulse to develop is evident everywhere, with everyone. I never see Wally Kozak, former Canadian national team ice hockey coach and currently a scout for the women's team, without walking away with something: an idea, an article, a question, a book, some reinforcement, a quote, something to reflect on. (On at least two occasions I've also walked away with a toasted tomato sandwich made from tomatoes that he had grown!) Marlene Rankel, an education-psychology professor who introduced me to Kazimierz Dabrowski, was the same—I always came away from encounters with her feeling somehow enriched. Leadership for these people truly is a mantle, a cloak they put on that transforms others. The very good ones can't help themselves. They are people who make a difference.

Are You a Leader?

Is this something that interests you? Can you, or do you, get caught up in the puzzle that is another person—and how you might encourage that drive you see in them, or unlock that resistance, or deal with that lack of confidence, or curb that overconfidence without breaking the person?

Here's a simple but practical way of beginning to see the challenges involved in developing others: a diagram that plots "confidence" (from low to high), on one axis, against "know-how" (also from low to high), on another, producing the following four quadrants:

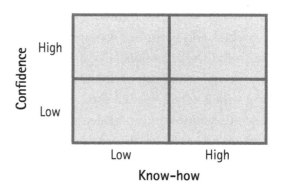

How could you best lead and develop people in each of these quadrants? Which group would be the hardest to coach? You might ask me at this point: "What do you mean by 'hardest'?" Good question. Some of you may relate very well to the low-confidence and high-know-how group because perhaps you were like that, or your best friend or one of your children is like that, so you have some affinity for these people and their issues. Other readers, those of you who came out of the womb confident, are probably thinking, "I can't relate at all. If you're afraid or fearful, so what—just do what I do: focus on what you have to do and don't worry, because worry is a waste of time!" Clearly, the degree of difficulty will vary depending upon the leader's background, experience and confidence level.

Do you like to ponder over the various people in your work world and the diversity of challenges they present? Do you think of yourself as a leader with a strong developmental bias? You may not even have considered this approach because the experiences that led you to become a manager or leader haven't prepared you for the job.

I spend a lot of time working with leaders and managers in the oil industry, most of whom are engineers or geologists. A few years ago I was working with a major company in the industry in the middle of its third downsizing. I asked the engineers in the room how many articles they had read during the past year on engineering or issues related to it. Their answers ranged from a low of 15 to a high of more than 100. I then asked them how many articles they had read on managing people through difficult change and transition. Not a hand went up in the room, and yet this was the very leadership issue they were tasked with. This was now their job. They were no longer solely engineers; they also had the responsibility, as leaders, to help their people through this difficult time.

A novice's view of leadership can be very restricted and based primarily on what they see on the organizational chart. When I was a young coach, I thought coaching was all about the Xs and the Os. I focused on creating the best strategy and designing the best plays. It took me a few years to discover that when you put a name on every X and O, things change dramatically, and suddenly the need for developmental skills becomes obvious.

Here is a diagram of the perfect executive team from Corporation B.

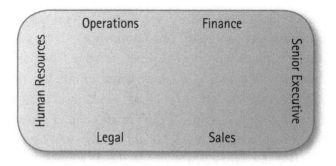

As the leader of this executive team, what will be your biggest challenge? That depends a great deal on who will be representing each of these functions. If it's Sally from sales, it's a breeze—she brings terrific team and communication skills to every team on which she is placed. Shawn, on the other hand, who also works in sales, is outspoken and at times too domineering in group situations. The point here is that the executive team works perfectly—on paper—until we start bringing the people into the equation. Then everything changes for the leader.

It's All About the People

Early on in the two-day corporate coaching workshops that my company, Performance Coaching, offers, we emphasize that there are three things that make coaching unique as a management style: a strong developmental bias, personal contact and caring. I then ask, "Why coaching? Why now?" In other words, why would a leadership style that emphasizes developing people through personal contact and caring be right for your organization, given what it is going through? In every single workshop, the first response on the flip-charts is some variation on "People are our primary resource." In the end, it's all about the people—and the relationship between the leader and his or her people.

What I'm suggesting is that the very best relationship you can establish with your people is a developmental one—one where, through your own drive and desire, you're igniting their Third Factor. You're inspiring them to want to be the best they can be (salesperson, accountant, custodian, CFO . . .), and also to continue to grow and develop as a person. There are many good organizational reasons for doing this, as well as moral and ethical ones. We cannot always guarantee people employment, but we ought to be able to guarantee that they are employable.

So let's talk about igniting your Third Factor and becoming a leader with a strong developmental bias who is very effective at growing and developing others. If this interests you, what's blocking you? What do you need help with? Is your biggest block around what to do and how to do it? Then you're in the right place; showing you how is the primary purpose of this book.

Caring is at the heart of really good leadership. To quote the message I once saw on a billboard in Cedar Rapids, Iowa, ". . . people want to know how much you care, before they care how much you know."

Any journey is difficult without accurate maps. This book provides you with the maps you will need to begin the process of becoming a leader who not only is very good at developing others but derives personal satisfaction from doing so. It's an endeavor of the highest order.

———————————

Editor: A rousing start, but there must be more to the concept of the Third Factor than you're disclosing here.

Author: Yes, a lot more in terms of Dabrowski's theory of moral and emotional growth, which he called the Theory of Positive Disintegration. He believed that if people had certain, what he called "over-excitabilities"— intellectual, emotional, sensual, psycho-motor, imaginative—they had the inner capacity to transcend their upbringing and culture and move to higher levels of development. The disintegration is positive: although the person temporarily disintegrates, questions what they are going through, and experiences what Carl Jung called "the long, dark night of the soul," they reintegrate at a higher level as a result of those over-excitabilities.

Editor: That's out there. How did he arrive at such a theory?

Author: Oh, that's a very long story. The short version is that he looked at the lives of those who most would agree had evolved to very high levels morally and emotionally, and saw that they had all gone through this process of temporary disintegration and then a higher level of integration. He wrote numerous psychological developmental biographies on such people as Kierkegaard, Christ, Gandhi and Martin Luther King.

Editor: That's interesting. Tell me more about the over-excitabilities.

Author: Dabrowski had another term for over-excitabilities. He called them "tragic gifts."

Editor: Why so?

Author: He called them gifts because, for example in the case of emotional over-excitability, these people really feel the world. They are in touch with all the joy and the suffering; they experience at an emotional level all that they and others are going through. He called them tragic because the world was not yet ready for people who felt at such a deep level.

Editor: When I was younger I read a book called There Are Men Too Gentle to Live Among Wolves.

Author: I know the book, and it's a beautiful example of what we are talking about. Now tell me: how do you feel about what we have covered so far?

Editor: There is hope.

Author: On that ringing endorsement, let's move on.

1
Developing a Developmental Bias, or a 3 a.m. Wake-up Call

Editor: So where to now?

Author: I thought I'd talk a bit about how this focus on developmental bias evolved and led to the five "rings" we'll be discussing in the book, and why this is important in the business world.

Editor: Hmm ... I've been thinking ...

Author: Oh-oh! Every time Sandra, my wife, says "I've been thinking" I know something is about to happen or change for me.

Editor: That's because wives often have a strong developmental bias as far as husbands are concerned, and that's what I was going to point out. The wife thinks: "I see so clearly where he needs to get better. Why doesn't he get it?"

Author: I want to point out that getting married does not often lead to the type of developmental bias of which I'm speaking. Sandra, for example, has clearly identified countless ways for me to be better. Observing my many and obvious flaws, she sees my need to be better in an increasingly wide variety of settings. I would suggest, however, that most of it is more connected to the fact that when we're out in public together, she doesn't want in any way to be associated with, or embarrassed by, any quirky behavior on my part.

Apparently this is quite a common pattern. Peggy Baumgartner, head of our training division, recently asked her husband, Richard, to write a self-assessment, an exercise we use in many of our workshops. When Richard scored low on the "self-critical" scale, Peggy couldn't understand, given his many and obvious faults, how he could be so blind. His response, she tells me, was that he had no need for such self-reflection, since she pointed out his flaws and shortcomings with some frequency!

Editor: I don't know Peggy but I sure can see her point. At any rate, perhaps my way of pointing out my husband's shortcomings could use some work. Let's hear if there's anything of value in what follows.

Author: Quit buttering me up . . .

You could have cut the tension with a knife. The finalists for the 100 meter hurdles at the 2004 Olympic Games in Athens were in the blocks. The world champion and gold medal favorite, Perdita Felicien, was in lane 5, and the hopes of a nation were riding on her. The gun sounded, and Perdita shot out of the blocks toward the first hurdle. She hit the hurdle, went down onto the track—and in a second her dream was shattered, along with the dream of the woman in the next lane, who fell over her.

I was asleep in my bed in the Olympic village by the time my room-mate, Gary Winckler, returned from the track events of the evening. He tried not to wake me as he fumbled around in the dark, but I rolled over and muttered, "What a bummer, Gary."

"Yes," came the reply, "but it will make us stronger." Gary was Perdita's coach.

In my role as a sport psychologist, I have worked with and coached hundreds of coaches. Gary, who is also the head coach for women's track and field at the University of Illinois, is an example of one of the exceptional ones. A scant few hours after what could have been a career-defining disappointment, he had already reframed the situation and was laying the necessary groundwork for recovery. His strong developmental bias—evident in his quest to ferret out the possibilities for growth in a bleak situation—was already in play.

Coaches come in all shapes and sizes, and with a range of personalities. But what the very good ones all have in common is that they operate on a similar set of beliefs and principles. Beneath the different personalities and the widely varying situations in which they work, the five characteristics of a developmental bias are very much in action. The same is true of exceptional business leaders and parents. A strong developmental bias underscores everything these people do. Their view of the concept of performance is much broader than athletic prowess, quarterly sales figures, or good grades. It is concerned with the whole person and that individual's development as a human being.

I first heard this "bias" expressed by the famous UCLA basketball coach John Wooden, at a seminar I attended in 1971 when I was a university basketball coach. Over the years, Wooden's teams at UCLA won 10 national championships—seven in a row at one point. (No one else has come close; the next highest is two in a row.) Yet despite his brilliant successes, Coach Wooden always maintained he would not know how good a coach he had been until at least 20 years after his last player graduated and he was able to see what they had done with their lives. As I write this, Coach Wooden is still observing—in his 97th year!

Let's further expand on exactly what I mean by a strong developmental bias so you can begin to see how you could tap into the Third Factor of the performers in your world.

Developmental bias is a new term that juxtaposes what is often perceived as a negative term—*bias*—with a decidedly positive one—*development*. But one can be biased in a positive sense, as in, "He had a bias toward always being honest, no matter what the circumstance." I could just as easily have used the phrase *developmental prejudice*, but the word *prejudice* has even more baggage attached to it. To be prejudiced toward a person's growth, success, well-being or development is a very good thing for any manager to have, but I settled on the word *bias* because it suggests a kind of listing in a certain direction, like a car with steering that pulls slightly one way.

Good leaders are always skewed to the developmental side even while trying to produce "straightforward" results. They get the results, but they develop the person in the process, so that the achievement of those results—or even higher results next week, next month or next year—is possible.

Managers with a strong developmental bias are not mean or dictatorial. They are just very passionate about their people using all of their talents and abilities. They hate to see talent go to waste. They are like my high school English teacher, Mrs. Lockyer. She knew what you were capable of and insisted on holding you to that standard. This is the essence of the developmental bias. And in exceptional coaches, it's like gravity—always there, exerting a pull, influencing everything a coach does. In good coaches, developmental bias supersedes everything.

I know that it was teachers like Mrs. Lockyer, who had a strong developmental bias, who had the most influence on where I am now and what I am able to do. I can also list the bosses and coaches I've had since my high school days who exhibited this bias with ease: they are those who have had the biggest impact on my abilities and beliefs. They are the ones who ignited my Third Factor, my desire to be more or better or different than I was.

In talking to and working with other exceptional coaches, I became more and more aware that this strong developmental bias was a major undercurrent in each and every one of them. It also became clear to me that there were five main principles at work in the service of developing their athletes.

In Search of the Developmental Bias

I can honestly say that until that 3 a.m. conversation with Gary, I really hadn't given any thought to writing another book. But in the ensuing days, as the Olympics progressed, the outline for what you will read here slowly emerged. It was clear to me that there are some exceptional coaches, and that leaders of all types—managers, parents, other coaches—could learn a great deal from them.

This wasn't a new idea in the sense that I've been teaching coaching skills for years. What Gary triggered in me was the desire to go beyond the obvious, to get beneath the surface and uncover what the coaches *did*. What was it about them or their style that made them so good for the people they coached, and so successful? Given all the experiences

I have been fortunate enough to be part of—including six Olympic Games and numerous world championships—I felt I was in a unique position to identify and convey those lessons.

I also have one other advantage. As an instructor in the executive development programs at Queen's School of Business in Kingston, Ontario, and as a trainer with my own company, Performance Coaching, I spend much of my time working with leaders in organizations. It has given me a clear understanding of the demands placed on everyday leaders. I could easily see that the leadership lessons from this "performance laboratory" called the Olympics also applied in the so-called real world.

In the process of writing this book, I first laid out the five characteristics of a strong developmental bias that I had observed in great coaches: that is, the five sets of behaviors they used to translate their developmental bias into results. Then I interviewed Olympic coaches and got them to comment on the principles and give their views. The coaches I selected were recommended to me by a few for whom I have had tremendous respect over the years. You'll get to meet these men and women in the main body of this work.

Once I had collected the data from the coaches, I put together a presentation on the five principles and took it on the road, to corporate audiences across Canada and the United States, to get feedback on the applicability of the concepts for everyday leaders. This book is the result of that feedback.

Go Deeper

We have developed a website in conjunction with this book so that you can assess yourself in each of the five areas as well as get some coaching on key skills. Go to www.ignitingthethirdfactor.com. Your username: perform. Your password: lead.

What follows is a summary of each of the five characteristics of a developmental bias to whet your appetite for what's to come. Over numerous presentations, I have arrived at the "five rings" diagram, which I find appropriate since so much of the wisdom contained in these pages comes from Olympic coaches and athletes.

Manage Yourself

People cannot move to high performance if they have to spend time and energy adjusting to you. Coaches are human. Even those with a strong developmental bias and the best intentions can sometimes get in their own way when they are coaching and developing others. In Chapter 3: Manage Yourself we talk about the tools you can use to be a more effective leader at critical times. Being skilled at managing yourself is a precondition to being able to access your developmental bias. This is especially true when you're under pressure, feeling rushed or uncertain—which pretty much describes the work world every day!

Build Trust

Here is what Olympic decathlon coach Andy Higgins had to say about building trust: "Robert Frost said it better than I can. . . . It's putting our belief into them so that they can have a belief they can use until they acquire their own." Wow. I had to read that several times to get the full impact of it. There are many other aspects to trust, of course, including competence. No matter how nice someone may be, or how much they say they believe in you, you will not trust them if you don't feel they are knowledgeable or competent enough about the area you are engaged in to give that kind of reassurance. We cover this in much more detail in Chapter 4.

Encourage and Use Imagery

Chapter 5 outlines one of the most powerful tools great coaches use: the language of imagery to create clear pictures for their performers. Imagery is the language of performance. People can't do things they can't imagine. The potential for development here is huge.

Uncover and Work Through Blocks

The fourth characteristic is all about dealing with the blocks that inevitably come up when developing others. When you are trying to get better at something, you are going to run into blocks. In Chapter 6 we discuss how to uncover the blocks in the first place and then build the performer's commitment to deal with them.

Embrace Adversity

In Chapter 7 we look at how exceptional leaders and Olympic coaches take an active role in situations of adversity to ensure that the adversity is channeled in a developmental way. When you have prepared for adversity, you're able to deal with it when it arrives—as it surely will. Choosing to be in the competitive arena in any endeavor means that sooner or later you will face adversity. It's the nature of the game. In today's business climate, for example, with its frequent and fast-paced changes, mergers and downsizings and unexpected setbacks, learning to turn adversity to advantage and ride the waves in a storm is an essential survival skill.

Interrelationships Among the Five Characteristics

We're going to talk about each of these characteristics separately, but in reality they are intertwined. They are like the ingredients in a cake: they combine in interesting ways that change them and make them into something more than they could ever be as separate entities. You can't effectively extend trust, for example, until you learn to manage yourself (and particularly your ego). It won't be possible to allow someone to do something their way unless you are prepared to let go of the conviction that only *you* know how something ought to be done.

The Tough Lab of Sport

Sir John Whitmore made some interesting comments on sport as a "developmental" laboratory. "Because sport is compressed in terms of time, the emotions involved are much more intense, so life after a time in sport is actually easier because you have been there before; it's familiar territory. I never experienced an extreme of emotion in life, in terms of highs and lows—that has been new to me. I experienced all of them in sport." He goes on to point out, as Dabrowski did, the importance of emotion in development and what we are calling the Third Factor. "I feel some people go through life cushioning themselves from their emotions, and I think they miss something. It is the extremes of emotion that give you your deepest experiences in life, and sport did that for me" (p. xi, *Sporting Excellence*, David Hemery).

In *Paradise Lost*, John Milton argues that virtue is not virtue until it is tested. How well things work when under fire is a test of their value. It is hard enough to succeed in the everyday world, but in the competitive arena both coach and athlete are on display before large audiences, exposed to scrutiny, their performance continually analyzed, evaluated and critiqued. The more important the event is perceived to be (the Olympics especially), the greater the impact on both performer and coach. But even at a minor sporting event one can see how competition brings out the worst in many people. That's why the five characteristics discussed here are so important: great coaches and performers have demonstrated that they hold true even under fire. And if they work so well in the heat of competition, just imagine how effective these fundamentals will be when applied on a daily basis.

In some organizations, particularly those where there are engineers, hi-tech people and others who pride themselves on being practical and task-oriented and on "getting things done," there is a stigma attached to the so-called soft skills. Developing others, coaching, and other such activities are seen as "fluff"—not really connected to getting the job done, hitting the numbers or bringing things in on schedule. This is a misguided view. It's the so-called soft skills that produce the "hard" results.

The coaches I interviewed for *Ignite the Third Factor* were united in their view that their role was to develop those under their tutelage to the best of their ability, using all of each person's potential. But sometimes the developmental requirement calls for the equivalent of a kick in the pants. I am not talking about being vindictive, but of being willing to have that "difficult conversation" even when you'd prefer to bail. Confrontation is difficult for most of us, but the ability to face it and use it effectively is an essential skill in developing others. We will cover that skill in Chapter 7: Embracing Adversity, but it is also outlined in detail, for those who are interested, in Appendix B: When All Else Fails.

Unfortunately, too many leaders focus on the end goal, and more particularly on what it will do for *them*. For such people it is certainly not about developing anyone. It's only about getting results. In most environments these leaders and coaches have a very short shelf life. I say in most environments because in a few situations, such as college sport, for example, the performers are forced to adjust their game to fit the predetermined designs, plans and idiosyncrasies of their authoritarian coaches. Winning coaches in these situations are tolerated even if they are not developmental. They get to replace 30 to 35 percent of their "workforce" every year. Try that in *your* workplace!

Commitment and the Developmental Bias

There are other ways of talking about developmental bias. In his excellent book *Coaching for Commitment*, Dennis Kinlaw emphasizes that almost everything a coach does should be in the service of developing commitment in the performer, the person being coached. He is not talking about commitment to the organization, but about building in people a commitment to *themselves*—a commitment to develop their own talents and skills to the highest level possible, and to work for continuous improvement.

In her book *Leadership and the New Science*, renowned systems analyst and consultant Margaret Wheatley helps us see a broader and more comprehensive meaning of commitment. She talks about people in dysfunctional organizations, organizations that have been tipped into chaos by leveraged buyouts or dramatic downsizings. She points out that about 25 percent of people continue to work to a high standard, care about their results, and bring creativity and enthusiasm to their daily work. At first she thought these people were simply denying reality, pretending everything was going to be okay three months down the road even though they had no guarantee of employment. When she interviewed them, however, she discovered that something else was going on. These were the people who had taken the time to create a sense of purpose and meaning for themselves in their work and in their lives, so that even if the organization didn't make sense, *they did.* They were performing this way, to this level, because it was part of who they were as human beings.

Such inner commitment to one's talents and skills usually reflects the work of some very good teachers, parents and other leaders who have taught, parented and coached with a strong developmental bias. Often, it is reflected in the individual in activities such as continuous learning and working on blind spots.

It is interesting to observe this commitment in young Olympic performers. Over the years they take on more and more responsibility for developing their own excellence and their own training programs. When athletes are young, the coach almost always does this, but exceptional coaches early on begin transferring these responsibilities to their young charges. The really good coaches understand that their job is to work themselves *out* of a job. They believe that this is the true meaning of empowerment.

Marco Beaulieu, who works in engineering management with Bell Canada, was a student in a weeklong leadership development program at Queen's School of Business in 2007. During this program, offered four times a year, I get to meet many excellent managers and leaders. Marco told me the following story about the development of commitment and belief.

He was coaching 10- to 12-year-olds in minor hockey in Montreal. He had three important values he wanted them to learn during the year: sharing, teamwork and respect. He focused hard on those values and brought in a few people with the appropriate expertise to help teach such skills as power skating and shooting drills. One of these experts was Nancy Drolet, a former national team hockey player and Olympic gold medalist. Marco said the kids loved her. She spoke to them about never giving up, and it became a kind of rallying cry; they became committed to pushing through.

The team made the playoffs, and to Marco's surprise got to the final game against a team that had beaten them all year. "They never gave up," he said, "and we were tied 2–2 at the end of the second period in the final. Before the game I had bought a cheap hand-mirror with a handle. In the dressing room between the second and third periods I had all the players close their eyes. I told them that when I tapped them on the shoulder they were to open their eyes for a second and look at the picture of the person who would make the difference in the third period." He then went around the room and in succession tapped each player on the shoulder while he held the mirror up to their face. The players rose to the occasion and won the game 5–2.

I had Marco tell my students that story the following morning. I asked the class how many of them wished their son or daughter had a coach like Marco, and every hand went up. We all, as parents, rejoice when our children get a teacher or a coach who has that developmental bias. It's wonderful to have an ally as we raise our children in these challenging times, an ally who helps ignite the Third Factor in them.

We can see a good many of the characteristics we've been talking about in this one example. Marco knew what he was good at and left the skill development to others. He was an aware coach with a well-managed ego. He had spent a great deal of time throughout the year developing trust in his team. He had a clear image of the kind of experience he wanted to create for the players, and told me he met frequently with the parents to engage them and get them on board. He knew confidence could be an issue in the final, when they'd be playing against a team they had never beaten, but he stuck to his values and gave everyone a chance to play. Finally, at a critical moment, he gave each player an image of himself as "the one to make a difference." He believed in them, and in the end they believed in themselves. In all likelihood, none of these players will ever go on to play in the National Hockey League, but with great coaching all the kids and their families had a major-league experience.

Developmental Bias: The Business Case

If you don't have kids and aren't involved in coaching recreational sports, at this point you may be thinking to yourself, "Why was this book in the *business* section?" Don't panic. I spend 95 percent of my time working with managers from across North America, and I can assure you that what follows was developed for, and applies directly to, your world.

So, why might this developmental bias be so important for your situation right now? What are your folks going through that might make the five characteristics of a strong developmental bias an important tool in managing them? We've asked hundreds of managers this question in our corporate training workshops and looked at the research. While we've received thousands of different answers, they can largely be grouped into five categories of required adaptation.

Demographics

If this one surprises you, you are likely living in either a research outpost or 1985. From 2005 to 2025, the number of people of working age (15 to 64) will fall by 9 percent in Canada, 5 percent in the United States, and 4 percent in the United Kingdom. By 2010, 50 percent of the management workforce will be eligible for retirement.

The time of being able to take it for granted that workers will simply appear when you need them to fill a key position is long gone. In "Make Your Company a Talent Factory" (*Harvard Business Review*, June 2007), Douglas A. Ready and Jay A. Conger note that they have worked with numerous companies that have "been forced to pass on hundreds of millions of dollars of new business because they didn't have the talent to see their growth strategies through to fruition."

The other side of the demographics coin is a company's capacity to appeal to, and retain, the so-called Gen-Y employees. These workers place a high value on development. They expect developmental opportunities and are willing to switch jobs in order to get them.

If you focus on development you'll increase the likelihood of retaining the employees who are key to your future success.

Emotional Health

The mental side of health has recently become a prominent issue for HR departments in all levels of business. With mental health claims representing 75 percent of short-term and 79 percent of long-term disability claims, the cost of ignoring the emotional state of employees is massive: $3.5 billion annually in Canada for stress-related absences alone.

The most important variable in the mental health equation is the relationship employees have with their direct supervisor. Managers who focus on development using the five characteristics of a strong developmental bias send a message to their employees that they are valued, that their voices are heard, and that they will be given opportunities to use their talents and improve. This directly addresses many of the key sources of workplace stress, including the most important: a perceived lack of control.

Moreover, if employees feel valued and cared for, they will value and care for their colleagues, customers and teammates. Just as stress promotes stress, so too does caring promote more caring.

Performance Expectations

Simply put, last year's numbers won't do this year. The competitive climate often requires departments and individuals to hit ever-higher targets with smaller budgets and fewer resources. The reality is that the only sustainable way to accomplish this is to focus on making the people you rely on produce better results.

The "Hallmarks of Leadership Success" report by the Corporate Leadership Council stressed that "above all else, top-tier leadership organizations are distinguished by their cultures of development. Central to these cultures are senior executives and managers who believe in employee development and act on these beliefs."

An article entitled "Executive Coaching as a Tool: Effects on Productivity in a Public Agency," published in *Public Personnel Management*, showed that training increases performance by 22 percent, but training combined with coaching increases performance by 88 percent.

Constant Change

Change is accelerating. With time-to-market shrinking, and many products being beaten to market by their own knockoffs, the ability to respond quickly and decisively to changes in the competitive landscape and to competitors' moves is widely acknowledged as a critical organizational competency. The only way to build this capability at an organizational level is to deal more effectively with change at the individual level. That means less "foot-dragging" and being on board sooner. And yet, this ability to adapt to change isn't something that can be accomplished by sending everyone to a workshop, seminar or conference; it needs to be built up slowly and thoughtfully through a one-to-one relationship between aware managers and their people.

Your Own Third Factor as Coach, Leader or Parent

So far, we've been focused on the "other person," but what about you and your Third Factor? In reality this book is all about my trying to ignite your Third Factor, about getting you interested in developing or expanding your developmental bias. What's in that for you? I am always surprised in our workshops at how focused the managers are on their organization and on their people. It is rare that leaders mention what's in it for them. I like to emphasize how satisfying it is for leaders to take on a developmental bias. It is much more fulfilling to develop people than to manage or supervise them. You are, in effect, leaving a legacy.

The Bottom Line

Improving your people will result in payoffs in the five areas above, as well as directly to your organization's bottom line. According to the McKinsey report "War for Talent 2000," "A-level performers deliver a 50 to

100 percent advantage over average performers in productivity, quality and revenue."

Join the "A" Team

There are leaders with a strong developmental bias everywhere, identifiable by their demonstrated belief in developing others and engaging with them, not managing them, supervising them or controlling them. They recognize that each individual is in charge of himself or herself, and that their job is to create an environment where each performer will focus on that personal commitment and grow. They make a significant difference in the lives of others and, by extension, the significant others in that other person's life.

———————————————

Editor: Okay. I'm a bit clearer on the whole concept of developmental bias, its connection to the Third Factor, and its applicability to the world of work. When do we get to the "how to do it" stuff?

Author: Soon. The next chapter covers the communication skills that are essential in coaching others. Then we'll cover the five areas and finish with a summary. In Appendix B we'll outline the difficult task of confronting when things aren't going well.

Editor: I thought confronting was part of communication.

Author: It is, but it requires attention all on its own. I put it at the end in an appendix because it's instructional and contains a lot of information, and not everyone will be interested in it. I called that section When All Else Fails.

Editor: I sometimes open with confrontation. It gets people's attention and keeps them on their toes.

Author: I can feel myself rising as we speak. Let's move on to talk about communication skills.

2

Communication

Editor: Let me see if I've got this: this chapter will cover all the communication skills our readers will need if they're going to develop others—that is, ignite the Third Factor in their charges. These are important skills for parents, teachers, managers, coaches, or leaders of any type.

Author: The last sentence is accurate. These skills are like the laws of physics—they apply everywhere. The sentence before it is a bit misleading, though, in that this is not meant to be the complete primer on effective communication. Some excellent books have already been written on this topic, and I'll be referring to a few of them as the chapter unfolds. What we are going to cover here are three basic communication skills central to effectively coaching anyone in any environment.

Editor: Don't you think communication is critical in developing others? Shouldn't we be spending a bit more time on this?

Author: It is important, but we have to pick and choose, and because others have done an excellent job in this realm we're going to cover three key skills: asking effective questions, listening actively, and giving competent, relevant feedback.

Most of us don't need the same skill level as, for example, a counselor or therapist. It may sound corny, but first and foremost your heart needs to be in the right place; in other words, you need a strong developmental bias, because the person you're coaching needs to know that you care and are profoundly interested in developing them. If that assurance is present, if they know you are in their corner, then being able to employ some basic communication skills will more than suffice.

Editor: Okay . . . that's somewhat nebulous, but let's proceed and see what comes out of this. I am a bit of a perfectionist and don't like attempting things until I have all the information or am fairly good at it.

Author: You're not alone in that regard. I've caught myself waiting until I'm pretty good at something before I get started. Now, I'm not suggesting you blindly dive into things, but if you wait until you're perfect at something before you start doing it, you'll never start because you will never be perfect! I'm all for learning the basics and then getting things underway. In the past this has led me to further development once I understand the problems I encounter and for which I'll need to find solutions.

This is really connected to the concept of progression, which we will discuss in the Build Trust chapter. I remember teaching volleyball skills to high school physical education classes many years ago. Tradition at the time was to start with the teaching of the serve and move to the overhead volley and finally the bump, a skill used most often when receiving a serve. Later on, the set and spike were taught. The trouble was that you could never play a game until the first three skills were mastered. One day I started by teaching the bump and then having the class play a game where a throw over the net replaced the serve and where, if they wished, they could let the ball bounce once before they bumped it. On the first day of learning volleyball they were engaged in the wonderful game of one-bounce volleyball. Not only did it make the teaching easier, but the students almost demanded to learn the other skills, which I introduced one-per-week over the next month. If I had waited until they perfected all the skills before playing, we probably never would have gotten as far as we did. The early engagement led to a greater interest and desire on the part of the students to learn additional skills. I'm not sure how this fits here, but I just wanted to tell the story.

Editor: I'm also not sure if it fits, but it does seem to add something. Let's move on.

Because I have been a coach in many phases of my life—in sport and even more so as a leader and as a parent of four now-adult children—I tend to think in terms of how people learn and how they will use what is offered. The preceding chapters introduce new possibilities and some exciting concepts. Now we'll talk of communication skills, because this is the foundation for all that follows. There is really only one way to ply your trade as a coach and engage the Third Factor in those you are developing: through your ability to communicate.

All good leaders, teachers or parents would agree that the three skills outlined in this chapter are essential and very, very easy to understand. You no doubt will also grasp the considerable importance of acquiring these skills if you are going to be an effective "Igniter." Grasping is the easy part. I teach these skills numerous times every year and still fail to access them to any meaningful degree in some of my own challenging situations—especially in dealing with difficult people! I am so much better than I used to be, but I still have a way to go. It's important here not to equate "simple to grasp" with "easy to do." The good news is that there are only a few key skills to be learned, and I know you can do it. I am getting much better and so will you, but to be successful you must make learning and practicing them a priority.

What I'm referring to in this chapter are the fundamentals of communication. These are the workhorses of communication skills. The very best coaches communicate effectively because they have mastered the fundamentals. You can too.

Here is more good news: These communication skills apply in *all* situations. If you develop them, you can do anything.

It is my not-so-humble belief that much of the coaching/management literature unnecessarily complicates the whole area of communication. It makes much of the *styles* of communication—mentoring, teaching, confronting and consulting—but much more important than those labels are the skills *underlying* each of the styles. **If you learn to ask good questions, be an effective listener, give really good feedback and know how to confront your performers when things are not going well, you can do most anything.** In this chapter we focus on the first three skills and leave confronting to Appendix B: When All Else Fails.

Core Skills in Coaching

There are two core skills in the consulting style of coaching: asking effective questions and listening actively. I will speak mainly about generating self-awareness and self-responsibility—the "to dos" of the Third Factor. These dynamics lead to engaging the other person and motivating them to evolve to a higher level. It's obvious how these skills connect to igniting the Third Factor.

Ask Effective Questions

A question is much more developmental than a command because it leads to reflection and awareness and eventually to self-responsibility and commitment. This is not new. Plato and Socrates taught extensively using questions, as do all the Zen masters. Self-realization is developmental, and **to *discover* is superior to *being told*,** because it engages the

Third Factor. Self-realization generates in the person the desire to get better and to take personal responsibility for moving to the next level.

The information in this section is freely drawn from the exceptional work of Sir John Whitmore, a colleague of mine, and David Hemery, an Olympic gold medalist. John Whitmore's excellent book *Coaching for Performance*, written some 15 years ago, covers in much more detail some of what I summarize here. David Hemery has recently put together an extremely useful book entitled *How to Help Children Find the Champion Within Themselves*. It is written for parents, teachers and coaches who want to learn how to ask better questions and grow and develop the children under their care. Another excellent book is Susan Scott's *Fierce Conversations*.

Consulting is a style of communicating that did not come easily to me. Trained as a schoolteacher, I had learned how to do a lot of lecturing and telling, and only listened when it was absolutely necessary or when the other person insisted. It's really amazing that I have been as well received as a coach as I have, given this gaping hole in my communication skills. It says something about learning environments that many organizations still welcome someone, usually a so-called expert, who comes in and "tells." John Whitmore was the first to awaken me to the incredible potential for developing others through consulting, that I, with my dominant-speaker style, had missed.

The idea outlined in *Coaching for Performance*—that you could trigger self-awareness and self-responsibility in the other person simply by asking effective questions and listening actively—was merely intriguing at first. But it moved quite quickly out of the intellectual realm and into the practical one when I was suddenly and unexpectedly called on to participate at the World Synchronized Swimming Championship in Zurich, Switzerland, as a performance coach in sport psychology with the Canadian team. I was at home packing my bags in preparation for the trip when the phone rang. Sheilagh Croxon, former Olympic coach, informed me that neither assistant coach would be on the flight that day due to medical issues, and that I was to tell the head coach, Biz Price, when I got to the airport. When I gave Biz the news, she said to me, "I guess you're it!" Was my skinny, six-foot-three, 160-pound frame, which had little synchronized swimming experience (as a swimmer, at least), *ready* for this?

Fortunately for me, synchronized swimmers spend a fair amount of time underwater, and while they were down there, Biz would turn to me and say things like "Jessica is on her nose." I took that to mean she wasn't straight up and down in her spiral, but to be on the safe side I simply said to Jessica, "You're on your nose," and when she agreed, "Yes, I felt that," I would ask a question like "What normally causes you to be on your nose?" And after the explanation, I would ask, "What sorts of things might you do to correct that?" Jessica would self-correct, Biz would glance over and comment that it was much better, and when Jessica came up for air I would tell her, "That's a lot better!"

This went on for a few practices until reinforcement assistant coaches arrived. I might add that for the first few practices the swimmers were amazed at how much I knew about synchronized swimming! My cover was blown when one of the swimmers was above water and heard Biz give me the correction. But that didn't matter, because in the meantime I had made the discovery that asking them how they thought they had performed a particular action and, if it wasn't to their satisfaction, how they would improve on it, was an amazingly effective style of coaching. There is tremendous power in asking effective questions and then being fully present—actively listening—for the response.

Nothing focuses attention like a question. I first learned this when I was teaching tennis. For 10 years I ran a tennis school in Toronto, and like most tennis instructors I was constantly telling people to watch the ball. It wasn't until I attended a workshop with Timothy Gallwey, who wrote *The Inner Game of Tennis*, that I clued in to the fact that if I wanted the students to focus on the ball it was better to ask questions about the ball than simply to give them the command to "watch the ball." When I started asking questions like "Which way is the ball spinning when it hits the ground?" or "What type of ball are you hitting?" I made the startling discovery that in order to answer my questions, they had to watch the ball! It wasn't the command "watch the ball" that focused attention, it was a question—and as long as I kept good questions coming, they stayed focused on the ball.

This is as true in business as it is in sport. Questions such as "What were the figures on that last report?" "What could we do to further improve the service here?" "Where could we simplify this process?" "What do you think the impact of that will be?" "Where do you think we could focus our energies?" uncover new awareness and bring greater clarity to the issue. When you ask questions such as these you immediately begin to **build awareness.** Seeing things with greater clarity is often enough to motivate people to take more timely and effective action.

The other advantage of questioning is that it **builds responsibility.** If my only goal is to assign responsibility to get the job done, I could just say, "You are responsible for this." "You do that." But much better and many more purposes are served if I say, "Who will take this one on?" "How confident are you that you can complete this on time?" "Is there any element you are unsure of?" "What obstacles might present themselves?" "When can you have it done?"

When the primary interaction is through questions, it helps you, as the coach, to find out if the people you are coaching have clarity and are on track. The questions and their answers also give them influence over their own actions and ownership of the issue at hand. By asking questions rather than offering solutions you are also giving them a form of recognition, which can be much more meaningful than praise.

Because you are trying to develop self-responsibility and awareness in this other person, the words you choose and the tone and body language with which you deliver them will be important. **The most effective questions begin with words that seek to quantify—*what, when, where, who, and how*—**which you generally qualify into phrases like *how much, how many, how often.* When you are trying to uncover a block, solve a problem or implement a solution, the **one word to avoid using is *why.*** "Why" is ineffective in these situations because it pushes the person into defensiveness and analysis—two states that are counterproductive to what you're trying to accomplish. Instead of saying, for example, "Why did you produce a month-end summary like this?" use phrases such as "What were the reasons for producing the month-end summary in this new format?" By rephrasing the question you get some understanding of the thinking and reasoning behind what they did. You will see how they organize their thoughts. For a coach with a strong developmental bias, this insight into their inner world is invaluable.

Generally speaking, when using this more consultative style in developing another person, you follow *their* train of thought. If you think they are off course you simply ask another question: "In what way is this connected to what we are talking about?" You may discover from their answer that this actually *is* connected to the issue at hand. You may get some valuable clarity on steps that need to be completed before they can tackle the end goal. On other occasions when you ask the question, they may become aware that they are off course and get redirected back on course.

There will be other times when, to you at least, there is an obvious solution they have not mentioned. Again, because you are being developmental and trying to build self-responsibility and self-awareness in the other person, **don't jump in and immediately tell them what they should do**. Instead, choose to ask a question. "I noticed that you didn't mention X as a possible solution; are there reasons for that?" I cannot tell you the number of times I've asked that question only to discover that my "solution"—the one I thought of in the first 10 minutes of speaking to them—turned out to be one they had tried much earlier and found did not work. (In these instances I was always glad I had phrased it as a question rather than just blurting out my idea. Otherwise, they might well have thought, "Does he think I'm an idiot? If he could think of that in the first 10 minutes of our meeting, doesn't he realize I thought of it long ago?" and I would have lost their trust as well as credibility as a coach.)

Questions can be powerful, but use them wisely. Some common mistakes in asking questions are:
- asking a question when you already know the answer
- asking a question so simple that it's insulting
- sounding like a cross-examiner (tone of voice is critical)
- not really listening to the answer

Use questions to:

- seek understanding
- clarify for yourself someone's position or level of knowledge
- guide people in a certain direction
- build confidence, awareness and self-responsibility

I'm not suggesting that you never give a command or tell someone what to do. There are times when that is the most efficient way to communicate with someone, especially concerning a simple task. But **asking effective questions is the primary skill employed by exceptional coaches with a strong developmental bias**. This is how they develop people. Good coaches use this style of communication most of the time. In the chapters that follow, the skill of asking effective questions comes up time and time again.

Listen Actively

Once you ask a question, you need to listen well. **Listening is a simple skill that is very hard to execute**. This may be because we equate being in charge with talking. There is an illusion that if you are talking, you are in control. The only thing you are controlling, however, is airtime. If you really want to coach well, you need to know the person you are coaching, the issue they are dealing with and their ideas on possible solutions. The only way to get to know all this is to listen and observe.

If we respond to employees without listening, what we are doing is prescribing without having all the information needed to properly diagnose, and they may end up having very little faith in the solution. Let me explain. If I go to a doctor and start describing how I am feeling and outlining my symptoms, but I feel the doctor isn't really listening or doesn't really understand the situation, how much confidence will I have in the diagnosis? How comfortable will I be with the solution he prescribes?

Many of us tend to want to rush right into things and fix them without taking the time to diagnose and understand. Part of this deeper understanding relates to having real knowledge of the person, their idiosyncrasies and how they learn. Wally Kozak, former Canadian national women's hockey coach and current scout, has a quote on his office wall at Hockey Canada that reads, "Coaching and teaching require one to find out how the player is smart, not how smart the player is."

In a "normal" conversation, when one person is speaking, the other ought to be listening and focusing on what is being said. Each person, ideally, takes a turn, alternately listening and speaking. The whole process works well when this occurs. Unfortunately, many people aren't particularly good in the listening role—those who have a need to control, for example, or are in a rush, or have a high opinion of their own knowledge or intellect, or quite simply don't care what you think or have to say. These are people who do not possess a "toggle switch" for alternating between speaking and listening. Over the years their switch has become stuck in a more limited, self-serving range that alternates between speaking and waiting to speak.

These people—and some of them may have quite positive, pleasant personalities—will never effectively ignite the Third Factor in anyone. **Listening**—the act of being present to another human being with the intent of truly understanding what they are saying—**is an incredibly powerful act**, and it's a skill mastered by effective coaches. Passive listening—paying attention and nodding—may be helpful in some instances, but active listening is the skill of choice if you really want to take on the role of developing others.

The "Activity" in Active Listening

Active listening is not only about truly paying attention to what others are saying, but also—and this is the active part—about letting them know that you understand them. According to leadership expert and author Stephen Covey, seeking to understand the other person is the first order of business in active listening. A really effective way to do this is to stop the other person every once in a while and let them know that you "get" what they are saying by relating back to them, in your own words, your understanding of what they have just told you.

Active listening performs the following functions:
- communicates respect
- gives you insight into another person's thinking processes, blocks and ideas

- increases their self-esteem and confidence
- guides you in assessing what the next step should be for their development

Listening takes three forms:
- **Simple passive listening**: eye contact, nodding, acknowledging.
- **Active listening**: clarifying, probing, checking out that your understanding of what they are saying is accurate, seeking to understand. There are many blocks to understanding the message, which may include:
  - people not feeling free to say what they really mean
  - feelings being difficult to put into words
  - the same words having different meanings for different people
- **Keen observation of nonverbal cues**: Observation involves not only using auditory skills but also watching for visual and kinesthetic cues. Often what you're hearing does not match up with what you see and feel as you interact with the other person. Making that distinction and feeding it back to the individual can be very helpful to their development. For example: "Your words are indicating confidence, but I sense some concern or reluctance to commit fully."

Often, all you have to work with when trying to help someone develop is what you see and hear. Your ability to observe well and articulate to the individual those observations is critical. The most common errors occur due to "mis-hearing" or "mis-reading" what someone is trying to communicate. Their words confuse rather than clarify because they do not match what you are seeing, or they are inappropriate, out of place, or over the top. Keen observation and active listening—combined—are the most useful ways in which to ensure that
- what you think you heard is in fact what the person intended to say, and
- you are dealing with the real issue or needs and not some symptom or false front.

What follows illustrates how anyone can become an active listener.

I met Robert in a leadership program at Queen's University. Let me describe Robert by way of his results on the TAIS instrument, a tool we use with executives and elite athletes that, among other things, gauges how they pay attention and in what ways they are distracted. On the interpersonal scales, Robert scored 98 percent on his need for control (just behind Attila the Hun!), 99 percent for self-esteem ("I'm right and I know I'm right"), and also extremely high in extroversion (97th percentile). On all three communication scales (intellectual, negative/critical, positive/support) he scored above 85 percent. I don't think you'll be shocked to learn that everyone from all levels of his organization indicated on his 360 feedback* that he needed to learn to listen!

I should point out that Robert was an engaging fellow and well-liked by his colleagues and superiors despite his listening deficiency. I met with him for a 40-minute coaching session and asked him what he wanted to work on. He mentioned a small, obscure behavior from his 360 feedback. I let him know that I was more than willing to coach him in that area but asked, "What about listening?"

"I've never been a good listener," he replied with a laugh. Then he talked about his history of not listening, describing incidents from elementary school and the home he'd grown up in. He finished by saying, "Peter, I don't listen; it's something I've never been good at."

In the chapters that follow on imagery and blocks, we will learn that often what's in the way, what is blocking someone, is that they can't imagine themselves doing something. For Robert, listening was a monumental and unachievable goal. He literally couldn't imagine himself as a good listener. The goal of becoming a good listener was, for Robert, an end goal. It was a very big hurdle and would be achieved only as the result of a series of smaller goals, called performance goals. (If the end goal is the top of the staircase, the performance goals are the stairs.) We learn later that good coaches focus only on performance goals.

I asked Robert if he was willing to let me help him improve his listening skills. He said he was, but then added, somewhat skeptically, "Many have tried." We narrowed the goal down to giving people who report to him his undivided attention when they came in to see him in his office.

---

* 360 feedback is a process of anonymous feedback from direct reports, the person the individual reports to, peers, sometimes people from other levels in the organization, as well as customers, family members and friends.

I started the coaching session by asking him, "Who do you know who is an exceptionally good listener?"

He immediately responded, "Monique, my wife."

I thought, *Well, she has to be.* You'll notice I wrote, "I thought"—I did not say this out loud. I didn't know Robert well enough to throw out a quip at this early stage in our relationship. It was important to manage my own ego and curb my need to be clever and possibly contaminate the coaching environment. (We discuss the need for the coach to self-manage in the next chapter.)

"Okay, Robert," I said, "I want you to be you and I will be Monique. I want you to coach me in acting and behaving the way Monique does when she is really listening to you. I want to know specifically what she says and what she does that make her such a good listener." Then I walked to the other side of the room and stood with my arms crossed.

His first comment was "She wouldn't be way over there."

"Then where would she be?"

"Over here, closer to me and on the same side of this table as I am," he responded. I moved over beside him and started glancing around the room. "She wouldn't do that; she would look at me." I looked at him and then looked away. "Oh, she wouldn't ever do that," he said quickly, then added, "She locks you in. When you are here [motioning with both arms to indicate a narrow corridor of eye contact between us], you do not want to be caught looking anywhere else!"

This bit of role-playing told me that Robert was beginning to get it. He was starting to be able to imagine what good listening looks like. But he thought he was done. "That's about it, Peter," he said.

"But, Robert, how do you *know* she is listening?" I asked him. "What does she do or say that lets you know she is paying attention?"

After a few seconds of thought he said, "She grunts a lot—you know, things like 'aha,' 'oh yeah,' 'uh-huh.'" I asked him what function he thought those "grunts" served. "Well, she's with me, she's encouraging me and letting me know she's following along."

I then moved to the most difficult part, asking him, "How do you know she understands you?"

It took a few minutes, but eventually he said, "Every once in a while she says, 'Robert, shut up. Robert, shut up!' and when I stop, she says, 'Let me see if I'm getting this,' and she summarizes in her own words what I said. If I say, 'Yeah, that's it,' then she says, 'All right, go on,' and I continue. If I tell her, 'No, that's not it,' she asks me to go back and re-peat, in a different way, what I've said."

We had to tone down the "Robert, shut up" part, but by now Robert had a very clear picture of what listening to a person might look like. I asked him, "When people come in to see you in your office, do you think you could go around to the other side of the desk, sit in a chair, lean forward and make eye contact, grunt, and every so often summarize in your own words what you hear them saying?"

"Yeah, I can do that!" he declared. (He couldn't listen but he could do that!)

Robert's company probably spent a good $10,000 to send him to the leadership program at Queen's. If, when he gets back to work and some-one comes in to see him, he engages in the listening behavior described above, do you think he'll have a different relationship with his people? You bet he will! Coaching is all about the little things that make very big changes down the road. It's about the performance goals—what Buck-minster Fuller referred to as "trim-tab adjustments." If the *Titanic* had turned half a degree south as it left England, it would have been in an entirely different place days later.

Metaphorically speaking, it's as if Robert and I went into a darkroom and developed a picture of what good listening looks like. And as I asked questions and actively listened to his responses, we gradually created a picture of listening that he could imagine himself doing. The skills of asking and listening are very important ones for anyone who wants to trigger the Third Factor.

Give Competent, Relevant Feedback

Now here's a vital skill that has been worked over in numerous ways and made much more complicated than it needs to be. I read several books on the subject a few years ago, and when I finished I was more confused than when I started. My friend Diane Abbey Livingston drew the following simple diagram on a cocktail napkin and said, "Peter, it's not really that complicated. The fundamental principle is that you learn to **tell people what you feel, see and hear, and not what you think.**"

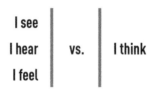

I see
I hear   vs.   I think
I feel

This was a brilliant piece of feedback for me on the concept of feedback. There are other guidelines, but learning to separate out what you are seeing, hearing and feeling from what you think—your interpretation—is at the core of developing your skill in giving effective feedback. And, boy, is that ever hard to do! I frequently teach this skill, and it is astounding how often I fall back into telling people what I think—giving them my interpretation. I was particularly guilty of this with my own children on the subject of the cleanliness of their rooms (or lack thereof!). I would fall back into using interpretive phrases like "You don't care" or "This is the biggest mess I have ever seen"—guaranteed, of course, to bring about immediate and lasting change in the child's behavior—not!

The truth is that when we give evaluations, the other party takes exception to our evaluations and rarely hears the message. However, if we are able to describe what we see and hear and how that makes us feel, it is far more difficult for them to dismiss our feedback. If, for example, someone pushes their chair back in a meeting, gets red in the face and starts shaking their head from side to side, my feeding that observable data back to them ("I saw you push your chair back, your face got very red, and you were shaking your head from side to side; what was that all about?") makes it very hard for them to argue. It's far more effective than offering up your interpretation ("I see you lost it in the meeting"), which they are much more likely to dispute. (You can add the feeling part if you need to let them know the impact they had on someone else.)

Let me say once again that this is much harder to do than it appears, especially when the feedback is corrective in nature. We are used to telling people what we think, giving them our interpretation of what has occurred, and it's a tough, tough habit to break. For most of us, capturing a group of behaviors under a single label is something we have done thousands of times. We are used to summarizing in our minds and labeling behaviors as rude, inconsiderate, evasive, uncooperative, bad, excellent, great, ineffective, et cetera. Not one of these interpretations, when fed back to a performer, will in any way enable them to get better at whatever it is they are doing.

The Four Rules of Effective Feedback

There are four simple rules for giving effective feedback. (I started with the second one, *describe versus evaluate*, above, because it is such a challenge.)

1. Be specific versus general.
2. Describe versus evaluate.
3. Focus on the behavior versus the person.
4. Maintain the relationship versus indulge in self-serving behavior.

The first rule, that **feedback should be specific and not general**, ties in with what we will talk about in the imagery section. There we explain that coaches need to paint clear pictures so that people can self-adjust their performances. Even positive feedback needs to be very specific if we are going to increase the performer's competence. General feedback like "You were terrific, Muhammad," or "That was a great speech to the Rotary club last night, Ashley" may make the person feel good, but it does little to improve their competence. How can Muhammad stay terrific if he has no idea what he did, specifically, that you thought was terrific?

The third rule reminds you to **focus on the behaviors you wish to improve**, change or reinforce in the other person. I recently asked a group of leaders in a seminar I was teaching if they thought their children were bad. Except for one jokester parent, all concurred that their children were not rotten-to-the-core bad. They also acknowledged, however, that they often were not thrilled with their children's behavior. I suggested that perhaps a more accurate form of feedback to their children might be something like this: "I love you, but I don't like the way you are treating your younger brother" (or the mess of your room or whatever behavior you're dealing with). The message then is that *they* aren't bad, but that you sure don't like the behavior.

In the same way, I may have an excellent employee with a bad habit I would like them to change. Let's say, for example, that one has a tendency to interrupt people in mid-sentence in meetings. It's the interrupting that I choose to focus on. "Adam, you interrupted Jacques three times during his presentation this morning. A rule of thumb in those situations is to let people finish talking before you comment or ask questions." If I think he needs to be made aware of the impact he had on at least one person, I might add a comment on my feelings: "I must admit I felt a bit frustrated by the interruptions."

In the above example I chose to take a teaching approach and did not assume competence on Adam's part—I did not assume he knew not to interrupt—and so fed back to him a picture of the appropriate behavior. Had I chosen to use a more consultative style I would have asked, "Adam, are you aware that you interrupted Jacques three times during his prepared presentation in the meeting this morning?" You will recall that the consulting style—asking questions and actively listening—is focused on developing self-awareness and self-responsibility in the other person. If he answers casually, "Yeah, so what?" then clearly he does not have enough awareness yet, so I might move to a second question: "Well, I know how *I* feel when I have prepared something I want people to hear in its entirety and I get interrupted. How do you feel when that happens to you?"

A third possibility is to use a mentoring style. Mentoring is simply coaching that focuses on a career path or survival in the organization. In this instance my feedback would sound more like this: "Adam, as you know, one of the things that is really valued in this organization is that we treat each other with respect and dignity. Interrupting Jacques three times during his prepared statement in the meeting this morning might be interpreted by some as disrespectful. I am sure that wasn't your intention, but I must admit I felt a little frustrated by it."

The fourth rule reminds us to **give feedback for one reason and one reason only: to help the other person get better**. Feedback is not meant to be self-serving to the person giving it. This is not where you get even or show them you're smarter. Whatever approach you take, you should be able to give feedback—all feedback—in a way that maintains the relationship.

If your feedback is to have maximum impact in bringing about increased competence on the part of the performer, then it should also be timely, varied and frequent. It was Paul Allaire, the retired CEO of Xerox, who once said that we under-communicate "to the power of 10." Just because we said it once doesn't mean people got it. For them to get the message clearly, you need to communicate it over and over again, as often as you can, in as many ways as possible. As for timeliness, research tells us that the effectiveness of feedback starts to decline 0.4 seconds after the act. The best time to tell someone? Now!

A few important final thoughts on feedback. **Leaders who are good at the skill of feedback are highly disciplined**; they think carefully about what they're going to say and how they're going to say it. Few of us can spontaneously offer up exceptionally good, competent, relevant feedback. This simply doesn't come naturally. All of us are capable of giving general, non-specific, focus-on-the-person feedback such as "Great job on that report, Bruce." Giving exceptional feedback is a different matter altogether. "I read the McDougal report, Bruce, and it's extremely thorough and well-targeted. It focuses on efficiencies, succession planning and return on investment (ROI), which are the customer's key concerns. I feel confident in forwarding it to the client. Excellent job!"

Who spontaneously speaks like this? Perhaps only your golf pro or someone who is trying to make you better. Most of us need to spend a few moments capturing the key points and getting back in touch with the guidelines for effective feedback before we're able to give such comprehensive, meaningful feedback.

Here's what University of Illinois track coach Gary Winckler had to say about the role of asking questions and listening in coaching:

"I ask them, almost on a daily basis, how they're doing, and I'm always telling them, 'Don't just tell me you're doing okay. How are you *really* doing, how's school, how's your family, how are you adjusting to homesickness?' It's not so easy, especially in the school environment, where you only see your athletes an hour or two a day and we jump on the field and do our routine and then go our separate ways again."

Gary is right. We do have limited time. But these constraints signal that it's even more important to make asking and listening priorities. If you want to make the most of the time you have with your people, take advantage of the opportunities you do have by using the most effective communication skills available to you.

It seems appropriate to finish this section with two simple questions related to your developmental bias and igniting the Third Factor in your people:

- If people continually come back to you for information, answers and feedback, are you developing them?
- What happens when you are not there?

Extinguishers don't engage the Third Factor in their people.
- They only ever *tell*—which often feels to their "peons" like *ordering*.
- They don't seem to have any real interest in the other person's thoughts on the matter at hand—even when that person may be the one with the data and the experience or the only one to have witnessed what took place!
- Their feedback, if they give it at all, is evaluative and has a "You should have done this, you idiot" feel to it.

To be an Igniter remember this!
- Ask effective questions. Engage with the other person and encourage their Third Factor.
- Actively listen. Be present to the other person and value their thoughts, observations and ideas.
- Give competent, relevant feedback.

Editor: That last question, "What happens when you aren't there?" is a doozy. It really gets at the crux of the matter.

Author: How so?

Editor: Well it would seem to me that if my answer isn't some version of "They would be as engaged and working as effectively and as diligently as if I were there," then that indicates that I, as the leader, have some work to do.

Author: It's a high standard, but given the quality of the work required to succeed today, it's a fair measure.

Editor: The piece on how to give effective feedback was very good, but it has been my observation that men in particular don't get the "feeling" part right. Men rarely distinguish between a feeling and a thought.

Author: I feel you don't know what you're talking about. I feel you are being very sexist here.

Editor: Exactly! Two good examples where you substitute the word feel *for the word* think. *Many of the men I know use the word* feel *as a synonym for the word* think *as if they meant the same thing.*

Author: I blame Bum Phillips, the old Texas football coach, for this. When he had Earl Campbell, the magnificent running back, on his Houston team, he would say in his wonderful drawl, "I feel like we can run the ball tonight."

Editor: You've got to be making that first name up—and I don't care who's to blame. A leader needs to recognize that a feeling is an emotion—I feel angry, upset, excited, et cetera—and feed that back to the other person to make them aware of the impact they had on at least one person, you.

Author: It is so a real name!

3

Manage Yourself

Editor: Manage yourself? Are we about to lecture readers on self-discipline or on some form of behavior modification or neurolinguistic programming?

Author: Exactly—and self-administered electric shock therapy for those who misbehave!

Editor: Get serious.

Author: One of my favorite quotes is from that famous philosopher Winnie the Pooh, who once said, "This is far too important to be taken seriously." Perspective is critical when developing others, and we need to be aware of our own inner world, our thoughts, our beliefs, and our impulse to react to external forces and events. Sometimes we want something so badly for the other person that we become evangelical about it and turn them off. At other times our frustration may interfere with what we say and how we say it. To engage another person in becoming more self-aware and responsible, in other words to engage their Third Factor, we have to create an environment where this can and will occur. The manager's or coach's ability to self-manage is significant, because they are the most influential factor in the performer's world.

Editor: My son plays minor sport and I hate how I feel and think at his games. Most of the time I contain it, but every once in a while I say something or act in a way I really don't like. It's hard to stop myself, even with my so-called awareness.

Author: I know. I teach this stuff and I still catch myself when I'm at a competitive event. Competition brings out the worst in many of us. It's not just reserved for minor sport but anywhere we believe we are "competing," or where the outcome is uncertain or there is pressure to do well, or where we perceive the outcome to be extremely important. If you can learn and practice the skills we'll be talking about in this chapter at your son's games, they'll also serve you well in other environments.

Editor: So this really has to do with internal "stuff" that gets triggered in us.

Author: Exactly. Think about those times you're unhappy with your behavior. To what do you attribute your "misbehavior"?

Editor: Well, in the case of my son's games, my frustration at what I think is a lack of focus or effort on his part, anger at the officials, coach or another player, my fear that he'll be disappointed if he makes a mistake . . . lots of things, depending on what happens, who is there and how I am feeling when I get to the game.

Author: You are a very aware person! Frustration, anger, disappointment, hurt—these are all internal, so we need to go inside to manage them. Learning to manage what's going on inside helps us perform better on the outside, which can only help us improve our own performance at developing others.

Editor: Hey, maybe this could help my golf game!

Author: Let's not get overly ambitious.

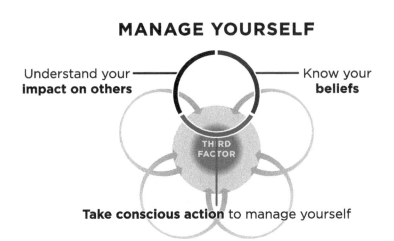

MANAGE YOURSELF

Understand your **impact on others** — Know your **beliefs**

THIRD FACTOR

Take conscious action to manage yourself

To develop others you must be awake and aware. It is challenging, if not impossible, for a coach to trigger the Third Factor in someone if they are lost in the emotional soup of the moment or caught up in some perceived injustice from earlier in the morning. Historically speaking, there was no one better at being "awake" than Buddha. He may have been the ultimate self-manager and Igniter!

After his enlightenment, a traveler asked Buddha, "What are you? Are you a man?"

"No" was Buddha's reply.

"Are you a god then?"

"No," answered Buddha.

"Then you must be a ghost," said the questioner.

"No," answered Buddha.

"Then what are you?" demanded the man.

"I am awake" was Buddha's reply.

This chapter is about waking up and starting to notice how little we actively direct what we do: how often we are at the mercy of what we are experiencing or what our beliefs are.

Knowing yourself is certainly part of managing yourself, but alone it is not enough. And awareness often leads to a change in behavior, but not always. For example, someone could know that they are behaving like a complete jerk and yet do nothing to change their ways. Regardless, awareness is the first step. If, for example, I ask you to become aware of your jaw muscles and to notice any tension there, you will probably relax the muscles. I don't have to stop and teach you how to do that. Once you have become aware of the tension, relaxing is to some degree automatic. But this is not true for all behavior, especially in the context of trying to develop another person.

Depending on your background, you may step on any number of landmines as you venture out into the developmental field. Some of them will be connected to your beliefs; others will be connected to your tendency to react to things you see or hear. These may make it difficult to access your developmental bias when it is most needed. What will become obvious is that these feelings, opinions and reactions are not going to go away just because you notice them. You have to become conscious of them to the point where you're prepared to take action to manage what you've uncovered. Only in that way will you move to "conscious competence." If you become extraordinarily good at noticing and then acting to deal with what you notice, you may eventually move into the realm of *un*conscious competence, or automatic expertise. But that isn't easily achieved. Even Mahatma Gandhi had to work hard and persistently at self-management.

The term *self-management* is somewhat misleading. It might be more accurate to talk about management occurring from the position of the Self. **What is unique about us as human beings is that we have the capacity to be aware and to self-direct.** I find it helpful to think about that capacity as coming from the Self, which could also be called the Observer. The Self notices what is happening and what we are experiencing, and steps in and redirects us to where we need to be. In the third section of this chapter we talk directly about the role of the Self.

If you are a parent, think about those times when you aren't at your best in dealing with one of your children. In the middle of an ineffective rant, have you ever noticed a voice inside you whispering something like "I can't believe I'm actually saying this"? Who is speaking there? It's the Self, the Observer, or, as Italian psychologist Roberto Assagioli put it, the Fair Witness. We all have this Self within us, and being able to access it, especially when under pressure, is critical if we are to be truly effective in developing others.

Here's a story illustrating how I learned this lesson—the hard way! I have always had a strong developmental bias and have derived a great deal of pleasure from working with and developing others. I went into teaching for those reasons, although I certainly wasn't all that good at it in the beginning. Early on I was much more focused on skills development related to the sport I was coaching than on igniting the Third Factor in the people I was coaching. Also, being fairly (some would say very) high-strung, I didn't deal well with competition. It brought out the worst in me.

In 1968 I was hired as a physical education teacher for a new regional high school in Shawville, Quebec. I had had exceptional training in teaching and coaching from a number of people at the University of

New Brunswick, particularly John Meagher, who to this day remains the single best instructor I ever had. We were taught the skills and then how to teach them—everything from how to demonstrate, where to stand in relation to the class, which way the class should be facing (e.g., back to the sun, boys' class away from the girls' class), to key teaching points such as progression and whole/part learning.

In our Friday afternoon coaching classes we learned not only from the varsity coaches at the university but from numerous guest instructors who coached the teams that played against UNB on Friday nights. As the university was close to the border, these included American as well as Canadian coaches.

I knew what to do and I'd been taught how to do it, but something interesting happened when games got tight and my competitive nature reared its ugly head. I reverted to coaching the way I had been coached back in the community in which I grew up. Every parent will immediately recognize this. We may read any number of books on parenting, but in a crisis it's astounding how often our mother's or father's voice jumps out of our mouth!

I was reminded of my early coaching days a few years ago when I was presenting to a group of executives. At the break a gentleman approached me and asked if I recognized him. I had to admit I did not, though the name on his name tag was familiar. It turned out I had taught him in high school. On the second day of the seminar he brought along a yearbook from the high school in Shawville containing three photographs of me that were embarrassing to look back on!

In the first one, I am in the middle of the floor at a basketball game speaking animatedly to the referee. (I should point out to non-sports fans that one does not coach from the middle of the floor in basketball.) In the second one I am being assisted off the floor by the principal and a fellow teacher. In the third, I am being escorted down the hall and out of the building. Being thrown out of the game, the gym and the school was not a high point in my coaching career, but it certainly was a wake-up call.

Now, if you had asked my players how they felt about me as a coach, they would have spoken positively. Most of the time I had a wonderful relationship with them. Unfortunately, I did not perform so well in the competitive framework. It took me a few years to transfer the coaching skills I had been taught to the high-pressure environment of the performance arena. I was not yet a developer of people; I was still simply a basketball coach. I didn't yet have a true, fully formed developmental bias. One of the key things I was missing was the ability to manage myself under pressure. This inability to self-manage was directly connected to my inability to access my skills and to get in touch with my purpose—what I was really there to do, which was develop the players—when I was under pressure. I was certainly not yet an Igniter!

This failure to self-manage can also be observed in the workplace. We may display excellent managerial and developmental skills when things are running smoothly. But how we perform when the deadline changes, a key performer is on holidays or off sick and a senior executive needs something *yesterday* is the true measure of our leadership and developmental skills. Coaches who can manage themselves understand the impact they have on others, are thoroughly attuned to their own beliefs and aware of how these affect their behavior, and take conscious action to ensure they are managing themselves at all times.

Your Coaching "Hats"

As a leader you wear two hats: one in your role as coach, and one in your role as performer. You need to be able to manage yourself in order to develop another person, but in developing the other person you also need to include the very skills you use to manage yourself! For example, if calmness is required, you need to use certain techniques to manage your own energy level while simultaneously encouraging the development of these same skills and techniques in the other person.

To ensure that everything we cover from here on is applicable to your world, I will use meetings and the leading and facilitating of meetings as an example in each chapter. As a leader you spend a lot of time in meetings of one type or another, and how you act in those situations reveals a lot about your beliefs and philosophy, your self-management skills and your ability to communicate. Meetings are also a great forum in which to display your developmental bias. As we'll soon see, there is much you can do of a coaching nature in these sessions.

Understand Your Impact on Others

One of the primary reasons coaches need to understand and manage themselves is that they have a dramatic impact on those around them. Of all the things in the performers' environment there is none so important as the coach. **If the performers are spending time adjusting and adapting to the coach** for whatever reason—the coach is moody, an ineffective communicator, or not a good listener—**it will be very difficult for them to move to high performance**. People cannot spend time adjusting to the idiosyncrasies or lack of skill of their leaders and still be exceptional performers. If your people are spending 10 to 15 percent of their time adjusting to you and the distress you create for them, they are unlikely to perform at their highest level.

As coach John Wooden once remarked, "Manage yourself, so others won't have to."

In a workshop I did with some of the top developers of people in the country (40 Olympic coaches), I divided the participants into four groups, each with a different time frame: three months, three weeks, three days and three hours before their athletes competed at the Olympics. I asked them to break down, for each of those time frames, how much time was spent on encouraging competence (making the athletes better) versus confidence (making the athletes believe they can succeed). There was 100 percent agreement that confidence was the most important factor in all phases—and that it became increasingly important as the coaches moved from three months to three hours before the competition.

I then asked them, "How many of you are perfectionists?" Lots of hands went up. So I asked, "What is your natural tendency as the pressure builds before the event? To become more perfectionistic, or less?" They could see where this was going but acknowledged that they would tend to be *more* perfectionistic. But what did their athletes need? Less, *much less*. Most coaches are very good at detecting and correcting errors, an important ability. But **without awareness, sometimes under**

pressure our greatest strength becomes our biggest weakness because we let our tendencies dictate our behaviour. We forget to manage ourselves.

Because it's so hard for people to excel if they are spending time adjusting to the coach and/or the stress the coach is creating for them, many of the coaches told me that they made a point of sitting down with their athletes and saying, "Tell me if there are things I do that irritate you," or, in the words of coach Debbie Muir, "drive you crazy."

A few years ago I was working with a media company at a resort north of Montreal. I was having lunch with two women who reported to a senior VP, and we were speaking French—or, more accurately, they were speaking French and I was listening. My French is not strong, but I get by. I speak what is called street French. It improves with beer—at least *I* think it improves with beer. There was no beer at that lunch. They were in the middle of talking about their boss when the conversation abruptly shifted to the weather and they laughed. I had obviously missed something, so I stopped them and said, in French, "I'm lost."

"Where did we lose you?" they asked in their flawless English.

"When you shifted from your boss to the weather and then started laughing," I replied.

"Oh," they said, "it's the same thing. You see, our boss is very moody, so if we have to see him we phone his secretary first and ask, 'What's the weather like today?' And if it's stormy and we don't really need to see him or it can wait, then we don't go."

The anecdote was funny, but is it *really* funny that these two competent women have to spend time and effort adjusting to this turkey? I think not. How can you expect people to move to high performance if they are spending 10 to 15 percent of their time adjusting to *you*? You may not be negative or dictatorial like this man, but perhaps you lack clarity, are unwilling to confront, or have some other blind spot that requires others to adapt, wasting valuable time and energy that could be better spent moving into higher performance. This man was clearly a better Extinguisher than an Igniter. He effectively put out any inner fire of the Third Factor in those under his leadership.

A few years ago, when I was doing a workshop with a team from a major electronics firm, we investigated some of the self-management skills that would help people perform better. The team decided to role-play a situation with the senior manager and one of the people who reported to him. The manager had his "mental preparation" plan, as did the employee. The manager told me his goal was to put the employee at ease and to create a relaxed atmosphere. One of the things he did while casually talking to the employee was to pick up a baseball he kept on his desk and toss it up and down in his hand, with his feet up on the corner of his desk.

In the debriefing session, both parties talked about their strategy. To a person, everyone in the room who reported to the senior manager said they hated the baseball toss. Some talked about it as a distraction, some as an indication of indifference, some as a symptom of lack of caring—the complete opposite of the boss's intention. If something this small has an impact, imagine the large, negative impact of a moody boss, or one who lacks the ability to provide clarity on performance expectations!

Managing the impulse to react is a big part of leading. This is critical in confronting, as we will see. It's also important on a day-to-day basis or before big events. Hockey coach Mel Davidson told me, "I really have to work on reaction, especially before a game because I'm so anal on the details and the channel of communication. I have to be very aware of my reactions—before and after a game—because I expect things to flow smoothly on game day and especially when we get to the rink and after. Sometimes I react more quickly and maybe more harshly than I should."

She went on to point out that you don't want to go to the opposite extreme of being too relaxed, because people may get the wrong message. "I'm also conscious of not being too light," she said. "Your support staff in particular can read that as 'Oh, this game isn't important'—especially in our situation, where we have games people anticipate we'll win regardless. So I have to be really careful. Whatever mood I want to portray in the important games is the one I also have to portray in the games they perceive as 'easier.' Your staff reads your mood."

Get Your Heart Rate Down

Debbie Muir, gold-medal synchronized swimming coach, talked about her response during the Los Angeles Games, her first Olympics as a coach. "It was two hours before the event," she recalls, laughing. "The swimmers were putting their hair up or something. I was in a tent by myself, and my heart was racing. When I took my heart rate it was 200. I always try to look calm and be normal for the athletes. The worst thing you can do at a competition is change the way you look or how you coach. So I had a bit of a chuckle and got my heart rate back down. I was just so nervous the whole time—really, really nervous—and when you get your arousal level up too high, you can't be effective because your decision-making process has become too flawed."

If you're interested in learning how to do this, go to the website (www.ignitingthethirdfactor.com) and practice the centering skill.

Engage in Positive Self-talk

What you believe about others and about what they need to develop will dramatically influence how you approach your developmental role. One way of uncovering your beliefs is to listen to the way you talk to yourself. Self-talk is generated by your beliefs and is supportive of them. Your perception is also supported and reinforced by your self-talk.

Statements like "There's no time to do this effectively," "My people prefer to be told what to do," "I'm not cut out for this," "They don't care," "It's easier to do it this way," all limit your effectiveness in leading and developing others. In Richard Bach's book *Illusions,* one of the central figures, the reluctant Messiah, points out that if you argue for your limitations, then in time they will be yours.

Examine your language; it will teach you what you believe and how you may be restricting yourself.

Mel's primary interaction with her players is during the game-day meeting, which lasts 20 to 30 minutes, and between periods. What about your meetings? As a leader are you aware of the impact you have on your "players," and do you consciously manage the message you convey with your body language? Do you ensure that people feel free to express their opinions on key agenda items? Do you create a high-performance atmosphere where everyone is free to give their best? These are tough questions, but as we move forward through the material, the "how to" of it will become clearer. If you can become effective as a developmental coach in a meeting environment, you will have moved a long way toward being a really good leader.

Know Your Beliefs

At the turn of the century a man named Louis Wirth said that the single most important thing we need to know about ourselves is what we take for granted. What assumptions are we operating on that we never question and assume to be true? In his book *The Path of Least Resistance,* Robert Fritz reveals that the roads in what is today the city of Boston were actually designed by cattle choosing the path of least resistance as they moved across the terrain. Those cattle paths eventually became dirt roads, then gravel roads and finally paved roads. His point is this: the only way to change what is on the surface, the roads, is first to change the underlying structure—what is supporting those roads. If you don't level out the hilly sections or fill in the valleys, the path of least resistance will be where it's always been. So too with us. The only way to change what we do on the surface—our behaviors—is first to go inside and change the beliefs that support those behaviors. Unless we change our beliefs, we cannot change our behaviors.

Here are a couple of questions for you to ponder. What do you believe constitutes effective coaching? When you think of a coach, what images and thoughts come to mind? Without being aware of it, you may hold a picture of a coach as an expert, someone who takes charge and provides answers, direction and a strong hand to those being coached. It is my hope that as you read this book, a picture of coaching will emerge that is more complete and "performer-centered."

A woman in the executive development program at Queen's University, while on a tour of the library, looked up the word *coach*. She came back with this definition: "a vehicle that takes people of value from where they are to where they need to go." Clearly a definition of a more regal, old-fashioned kind of coach, but accurate nevertheless!

Debbie Muir told me about her evolution as a coach and how she became increasingly aware of a restricted set of beliefs that she held about what she did. "I think back to when I first started coaching, and there weren't a lot of role models out there for me," she said. "I read an article, an interview with Don Talbot [an Australian swim coach], about how you just have to be the most hard-assed person in the whole world. Don't compromise anything; you've got to be tough. He became my role model, and for the first three or four years of my coaching career I was like that.

"I remember one swimmer in particular. Her brother was getting married on the Saturday and she wanted to go to the rehearsal dinner the night before. She would have to miss a practice. I said, 'No, you can't go. If you want to be on this team you have to be at practice tomorrow.' I was that sort of tough. For the wedding she was going to have to miss a practice, so I said, 'I'll let you go to the wedding, but now we are going to have our practice early in the morning so that nobody misses it.' I was so rigid. You're not going to get too far being like that. Eventually I figured it out, because it also wasn't my personality."

What you believe can dramatically restrict your ability to coach, even if your beliefs are based on past successes. In fact there are occasions when nothing gets in the way of future performance like past success. When we believe we have the formula, many things can start to happen: effort level drops slightly, we close ourselves off to learning and information in the competitive environment, we become myopic. We need to keep in mind that continued success—in sport, in business and in life—requires continual and ongoing adjustment to changing conditions.

Our beliefs determine our behavior, which in turn is tied to our performance. Therefore, a restrictive belief system leads to limited performance levels. In other words, you can't *achieve* success if you don't *coach* for success. You need to coach to the highest common denominator, believing that everyone wants to engage their Third Factor—all the while realizing that this doesn't hold true for everyone all the time. Your philosophy is vital to your success as a coach. Any limiting belief (such as "people want to take the easy road") can lead to coaching behavior that results in a self-fulfilling prophecy, or narrows the possibilities.

Your Philosophy Is Your Touchstone

The John Woodens of this world have a clear set of deeply held beliefs that are grand and inclusive in nature. Anyone employing them will realize success. The beliefs are well grounded in an understanding of human behavior and fit all parties who wish to get better. There are many building blocks and levels in Wooden's pyramid to success, all underpinned by a philosophy as full and diverse as the people he is coaching. Swen Nader, who played for Coach Wooden, talks about one aspect of this philosophy in his book *You Haven't Taught Until They Have Learned*.

> "Coach is . . . a stickler for fairness. But that didn't mean treating all his players and students exactly alike. In the 1930s, he came up with an approach he called 'earned and deserved.' To quote Coach Wooden: 'I believe that to be fair to all students, a teacher must give each individual student the treatment he earns and deserves. The most unfair thing to do is to treat them all the same.'"

Swen points out that his coach didn't just make that speech on the first day and then not follow through. Players who were late for practice, for example, but who had not only a good excuse but a record of punctuality, were allowed to practice, whereas others, whose past record wasn't so good, were dealt with quite differently.

We all need to be more aware of how our beliefs might be limiting possibilities and be willing to open up to new or different belief systems. Listen carefully to any coach or business leader for a period of time and it's easy to identify what they believe. Those with a strong developmental bias see possibility in everyone, ask lots of questions and really involve the performer. Less secure coaches and leaders, with a high need for control, generally don't have these tendencies. Expectation plays a huge role here. If you believe that everyone can succeed given the opportunity, your approach will be very different from that of someone who believes it's how you dress or who you know that matters.

One of the things I notice in attending coaching clinics is that there are always lots of "developers" present. They never stop learning. They're always in the process of "getting there," never believing for a minute that they have arrived. Knowing that they always have more to learn is an important part of their belief system.

Your philosophy is your touchstone. It makes the world more black and white at challenging times. Let me explain. Kazimierz Dabrowski wrote on moral and emotional growth. He believed that when we are young we often see the world as black and white, but as we grow we become aware that there are actually many shades of gray. We struggle with what is right because often there is no clear answer. However, once we have established for ourselves a clear hierarchy of values, the world once again becomes more black and white.

Coaches I have been speaking about—from John Wooden to Andy Higgins—**have a clear hierarchy of values.** They have a firm set of beliefs concerning their role as developers of others, and their developmental bias is grounded in these beliefs. These coaches are not going to compromise their values simply to win a game, or look the other way when a key player is not adhering to team rules. They are not swayed by what is happening moment to moment but are guided by their philosophy, what they believe. More than a few cases in recent history—from steroids in sport to the lack of ethics in big business—indicate that we need more leaders who have the values of exceptional coaches.

Beliefs, Half-truths and Paradoxes

One of the problems with beliefs is that many consist of half-truths. Take a common belief like "If it ain't broke, don't fix it." Is that true? It may be true if you're busy and have many things to do, in which case you'll want to focus on what most needs your attention, such as things that aren't working well, or at all, rather than things that are okay. On the other hand, few of us drive to town in a horse and buggy. There was nothing wrong with the horse and buggy—it wasn't broken—yet Henry Ford and others decided to "fix" it. As with many of our beliefs, this saying is true some of the time but not all of the time.

Often this creates a paradox: Winning is everything—and yet, it isn't. Decathlon coach Andy Higgins put it this way: "I consciously went to competitions reminding the athletes of this almost paradoxical thing of giving it the absolute best you can, but understanding that in the grand scheme of things it doesn't mean very much. Running around [the track] till you can't take another step and you're right back where you started—what was the purpose of this? If they were keeping score or measuring, did they want to win? Yes! But the most conscious thing I did was to keep this thing in perspective and to understand that what really mattered in the end was what happened to the human beings, their growth, and their process. The real value is not medals but who they become in the process."

James Autry, in his book *Love and Profit: The Art of Caring Leadership,* lays out his philosophy. He lists his principles on one side of the page and his corollaries on the other. One of his principles, for example, is "People will do a good job because they want to do a good job." The corollary opposite of this principle is "Not everyone wants to do a good job." What is the truth? The truth is that both of these are true, and it is the ability to hold the "all of it" that is important. The world is not black and white and neither are the situations you deal with. Sometimes you have to have a belief in a philosophy that you know does not apply to everyone in all circumstances. Some people do not want to be *developed*—and they will need to be *managed* instead. But if you try to apply that to everyone, you will severely limit those who, given the chance, would thrive under the tutelage of someone with a developmental bias.

Your Beliefs Affect the Performance of Others

When I worked with one large international consulting firm developing their young leaders in the skills of coaching, I was interested to see the performance reviews and how greatly they varied depending on the nature of the supervision they received in the organizations in which they were placed. This particular consulting firm had what they called "fly-back Fridays" on the third Friday of every month, when the trainees would return to their home city and spend a day with the partner they reported to in the consulting organization. For the rest of the month they were in a matrixed organization where their direct supervisor came from the client organization in which they were consulting.

It was revealing to see how consistently even exemplary performers, who had been given exceptional performance appraisals on numerous previous assignments, received much more mediocre reports when they were placed under restrictive bosses. Clearly, they were fenced in and severely limited in achieving their full potential by the restrictive beliefs of these highly controlling leaders. I also noted that the levels of achievement for those organizations fell well below those in organizations where the consultants reported to leaders with a style more in tune with John Wooden's "earned and deserved" approach.

Maximize Your Return on Investment

An understanding that **not everyone is coachable** also needs to be part of your belief system. Some people bring life issues into the workplace, and most managers are not skilled at dealing with those. This is why most organizations have an Employee Assistance Program. When you see a behavior in someone reporting to you that is permanent, personal and pervasive, unless you are a therapist you're not going to be successful in developing them. Likewise, if you are a parent and your child develops an eating disorder, you will need the assistance of a specialist. You and I do not possess the detailed maps required to give these individuals the kind of guidance they need to move forward.

As a coach you need to know where your time will be most effectively spent and get the best return for your investment. You need to work with people with whom you know you have a high probability of success. Research tells us, for example, that fewer than 3 percent of managers have ever turned someone who has been performing at a marginal level for years into a highly productive performer. Your most limited resource is time. So, work with the steady, reliable performers, the top performers and the new hires. The steady performers do most of the work and create very few problems, so they hardly ever get attention—at least individual attention. You ignore this group at your peril!

Many managers avoid coaching the top performers, sometimes because they are intimidated by them or feel the performers are already at their max. Nothing could be further from the truth. These people often have the biggest potential in terms of hitting the higher numbers.

The new hires need early successes and early wins, and that translates into at least an hour a day of coaching in their first few weeks, and 30 minutes minimum thereafter until they are settled and on board. It's amazing how many people have told me, "We do a thorough job of selecting and interviewing to get just the right candidates, and then when we bring them on board we ignore them or turn them over to marginal performers for training because we're so busy."

Take Conscious Action to Manage Yourself

In terms of focus, sport psychology differs dramatically from traditional psychology. (I discuss this in my first book, *The Inside Edge*.) Where traditional psychology, beginning with Freud, focused primarily on dysfunction, sport psychology, or what now might best be called performance psychology, has focused on uncovering what exceptional performers do on the inside—in their minds—that makes them perform so well.

If you are going to become mentally fit so that you can lead effectively under pressure, there are four areas you will want to work on: perspective, imagery, energy management and focus. We have created a website (www.ignitingthethirdfactor.com) to assist you in learning to use these skills. Mental skills used by elite athletes and coaches to manage themselves require practice to become ingrained, and therefore usable at challenging times. We will cover some skills here, but I encourage you to go to the website. Think of it as your mental gymnasium. Some of the skills, such as centering, for example, are easier to practice with a voice leading you through them.

Sometimes by changing an external factor, such as the composition of your team or a meeting time, you can improve the environment for all concerned. But **even when you cannot change external factors, you can still choose your reaction to them**. Most of the time you are not reacting to what is happening but to the story you're telling yourself about what happened. Reframing is about changing the story and acquiring the energy you and others need to persist. We cover reframing in detail in Chapter 7: Embrace Adversity.

I asked Debbie Muir what she did to manage herself.

"You know all the sport psychology stuff you do with athletes? Well, I did it all with myself. In the beginning it was just about learning things like the Jacobsen technique and how to relax, then the whole self-talk area and that kind of thing. It really evolved over the years to the point where I used imagery, imaging for myself how I was going to coach that day in training. Every day in the car on my way to the pool, I would imagine how I wanted to be that day and what I wanted my face to look like, how I wanted my voice to sound, and how I wanted the athletes to respond to me. It was one of the skills I used."

Debbie was quick to point out that the impact of pressure doesn't suddenly go away. That's where humor and your relationship with your people can carry the day. "The athletes used to tease me because at every competition I'd get this bright red rash up my neck to my chin, so I started wearing turtlenecks and track suits. It was a sort of joke. They'd look to see if I had my rash and then say, 'Oh, we're okay, Debbie's got her rash, we'd worry if you didn't!'"

How important is this ability to self-manage in today's high-paced work environment? From the studies on the impact of negative, out-of-control bosses on employee retention to research on burnout, there's evidence that the boss's ability to be human and aware and not act out feelings is critical.

The business world, like the world of competitive sports, can be a pressure cooker. Competition can bring out the worst in anyone. Good coaches are aware coaches, and aware coaches are those who continually strive to be better. Managers need to be able to manage not just their performers, but more important, themselves: their expectations, their personal tendencies, their arousal level—all of which directly impact their ability to read the situation, make good decisions, communicate clearly and effectively, and react appropriately.

Ironically, leaders choke as often as their performers. Success comes down to learning to manage what is happening on the inside, at the body, mind and feeling level, in order to perform better outside, in the office or sporting venue. Let's bring this to life with a few anecdotes and then cover the basic skills needed to develop better self-control and manage others more effectively.

Prior to the Torino Winter Olympics of 2006 I was presenting to a group of potential Olympic medalists and their coaches. I asked them how important physical fitness was for them at the Games. They said, of course, that it was incredibly important. I asked them how much time, on a weekly basis, they devoted to physical fitness. They all indicated that they spent many hours staying physically fit. Then I asked them, "What percentage of your performance at an Olympics is mental? How important is it to be mentally fit?" The percentages on the perceived value of psychological skills ranged from 80 to 100 percent. But when I asked them how many hours a week they actually *worked* on being mentally fit, the answers revealed that the majority did very little.

I am always amazed by these revelations. If you rate something as vitally important, why wouldn't you work on it? But, as we will see in the next paragraph, it's true not just for athletes. One primary reason for inaction is time, and a second is clarity. It is easy to imagine and therefore be able to complete physical tasks, but not so easy to imagine or complete mental tasks. My book *The Inside Edge* assisted people in applying key mental skills to the business world. These mental skills are critical if you wish not only to manage yourself but to move yourself internally to a place where you can enhance your own performance.

Raise Your Awareness—Then Act on It!

I once asked a group of business leaders how important self-control and self-management was for them. To a person they said it was vital that as leaders they be able not only to manage themselves but to appear strong and confident on the outside, especially in crisis situations—which, they pointed out, occur all the time in the current work climate. I asked them how many articles they had read, tapes they had listened to or seminars they had attended in the past six months to assist them in dealing with this challenge. Their answer, as a group, was a resounding silence as they looked around hoping someone else—*anyone* else—would answer.

Isn't it amazing that so few of us will make changes based on *information*? It requires a giant wake-up call before we will act to change things we know we should change or learn things we know we should learn. I really encourage you to work on the self-management skills in this section. They are life skills—and the sooner you use them the better all aspects of your life will become. Don't wait until you suddenly find yourself in a hospital bed to acquire this conviction.

Decathlon coach Andy Higgins had this to say about the need for awareness and self-management: "The better I knew myself, instead of acting out of habit, the better I became as a coach." He went on to talk about learning what he needed to do.

"The first recollection I have of this awareness was in coaching high school basketball and yelling at the ref . . . and being extrinsically motivated because that's all that mattered, despite the fact that I knew better. I would, on occasion, act like a goof, so my first conscious act was to speak to myself before a game about what I had to do—about what external actions I had to take. The first thing I had to do was sit on the bench, observe the game, and *try to be useful and model the behavior I wanted.* Anything like that requires such focus and will, because every so often I'd lose it."

The first thing I teach in this area, which I call Mental Fitness, is the skill of active awareness. There are four levels of awareness in high performance, as you can see in the diagram below.

Level 1: Unconscious Incompetence
Level 2: Conscious Incompetence

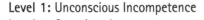

Level 3: Conscious Competence
Level 4: Unconscious Competence

The first level, unconscious incompetence, is **a total lack of awareness and action.** Years ago we were unaware of a lot of things—such as the impact of asbestos on personal health. We were unconsciously incompetent—that is, we didn't know any better. The same is true of our coaching. There may be actions we are performing now that are not good for the people we are developing, but until we know what these are, we really can't do anything about them.

The second level, conscious incompetence, represents **awareness without action.** We know what needs to be done but we don't do anything about it. We know we should exercise more, but . . . We know we should give better feedback, but . . . We know we should be more patient, ask more questions, floss more frequently, learn to relax—but, but, but.

There is a barrier between the second level, conscious incompetence, and the third, conscious competence, and the only way over that barrier is to act. "To know and not to do," said Chinese philosopher Lao-Tse, "is not to know." Knowing and understanding are not sufficient. We need to act.

At the third level, conscious competence, **we become aware—and we act.** When we are practicing and acquiring skills, such as the questioning, listening and feedback skills outlined in the previous chapter, we need to pay close attention to what we are doing and how we are doing it. I've mentioned that great coaches are highly disciplined, and a good deal of that discipline is directed toward monitoring, modifying and adjusting how they communicate with the people they are developing.

The fourth level, unconscious competence, is about **automatic expertise.** There are literally thousands of tasks you perform at this level—from brushing your teeth to driving your car. Sometimes even complex skills can get to this level—but not every time, even in the best of performers. There are days when Tiger Woods, for example, is "in the zone" (as this state is often referred to in the press), when he stands over the ball and everything is automatic. But most of the time he has to be consciously competent, fully aware of what he is doing and making small adjustments.

There may come a day when you are so good at giving competent, relevant feedback, for example, that it just flows out of your mouth correctly. However, it likely will take thousands of consciously competent repetitions to get to that stage, and even then, the odd situation will require conscious adjustment.

Often people expect that certain activities, such as dealing with others, will get a lot easier over time. This is not necessarily the case. Choosing to take on the responsibility of triggering the Third Factor in another human being is choosing to take on a complex and full mandate that may never feel any easier. But eventually—and this is very, very important—you become better at it and find it much more fulfilling.

The third level, conscious competence, where attentive practice is active, is the level we occupy most frequently when we are performing at our best. This requires that we learn the skill of active awareness.

Body, Mind and Feelings

Active awareness is a practical skill, not an intellectual experience. It is something you do, not something you know. The good news is that if you're alive, then you've experienced active awareness. Let's begin by taking a look at a simple configuration Roberto Assagioli developed to explain the key role of the observer within. Much of the thinking in this section is drawn from his lifetime of work in a discipline he called "psychosynthesis."

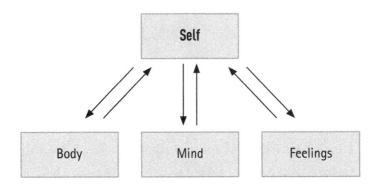

As human beings, and unlike most of our animal counterparts, we have the ability to observe ourselves—all of who we are and what is happening to us. By that I mean you can observe what is happening in your physical **body**—your breathing, any tension you may be holding, your heart rate, how rested or tired your body is, your tone of voice, and so on. You can observe things like what you're thinking, what your **mind** is paying attention to, how your thoughts change and how focused you are. You can also observe how you're **feeling**. Are you anxious? Excited? Happy? Sad? Lonely? Competitive? Angry? You can move to a place where you are able to observe your body, mind and feelings.

Your body, mind and feelings are the means through which you interact with the world. They are your personality—both what the world observes about you and the means through which you communicate who you are and how you want to connect. **They are not, however, all of who you are.** You are much more than these. This is something we frequently forget.

The body, mind and feelings are incredibly sensitive radar. They stimulate, enrich and educate us about the world and ourselves in relation to it. It is not unusual, however, for our minds to give us way more information than we really need or can assimilate. The mind sometimes becomes fascinated with an idea or event that isn't relevant to our lives or won't move us toward what we want to do. The mind may hold tenaciously to a belief system that is counterproductive for what we're dealing with right now. Our feelings often give us information we don't want to hear or don't know how to handle. The body often wants to do things it shouldn't or avoid doing things it should. This can result in a confusing jumble of sensations, images and thoughts.

Most of us get very little direct guidance or coaching on how to manage all this input. Basically it comes down to what we learned from observing our parents (our first and most powerful teachers), other role models we have consciously or unconsciously chosen, such as teachers, coaches, older siblings and society, and the norms or rules of conduct in the culture in which we grew up. Some of us have had great teachers; for others learning has been a dysfunctional nightmare. For most of us it's adequate just to be functional, but that isn't enough to allow us to achieve our dreams. It takes effort to develop consciousness about what kind of relationship you want to have with your body, mind and feelings so that you can direct yourself to your desired level of performance.

Stay on Course: The Role of the Self

Airline pilots tell me that planes are off course about 50 percent of the time due to winds and turbulence. But the plane has an autopilot that continually makes corrections, ensuring the proper flight path. Human beings are not equipped with this kind of autopilot. When we are off course, we have to make corrections the old-fashioned way, becoming aware and making manual adjustments to redirect ourselves. We've seen that the Self manages body/mind/feelings, but it also keeps us on course. Every once in a while we need to step back from our busy world, get back in touch with our vision and our role and redirect ourselves accordingly.

Let's suppose you see yourself as a developer of people, making a meaningful contribution to others through what author Peter Block referred to as "stewardship." It's hard to keep your role as steward front and center when you're caught in the tunnel vision created by day-to-day demands, e-mails, phone calls, meetings and all the other pressures of the workday. Every so often you need to consciously step back and make sure you are following your intended path, what you might call your vision of yourself as a leader. This, of course, requires taking the time to *create* that intended path in the first place. The famous American philosopher Yogi Berra once said, "If you don't know where you're going, you're bound to end up somewhere else."

The first thing you need to realize is that you are not your body, your mind or your feelings. Although you're getting messages from all three, all the time, they are not who you are. Your *Self* is who you are. One of the unique things about us as human beings is that we have been blessed with awareness. We have the capacity to step back and notice what we are experiencing, make a choice and act on that choice. We do not have to be swayed by, or driven into reacting to, what we are experiencing. This can be a challenging concept to grasp.

It Takes a While to "Get It"

A few years ago I was doing a seminar for some Olympic coaches, one of whom was cross-country ski coach Marty Hall. I was presenting the aforementioned concept on body, mind and feelings. Marty was struggling with the fact that I had said he was not his mind. As the class ended he was still arguing with me, convinced that he and his mind were the same thing, indistinguishable. We went for a beer and continued the discussion late into the evening and finally went home with the argument still unresolved.

The next morning I walked into class prepared with a new way to present the concept. "Marty," I said, "let me try one more time. I think perhaps you'll get it this time."

"It's okay, Peter," he replied. "I got it. There's no need for further explanation."

"When did you get it?" I asked.

"At 2:30 this morning," he said. "I was thinking about the concept as I got ready for bed, I was thinking about it as I got *into* bed, but do you think I could get my mind to shut up and stop thinking about it as I tried to fall asleep? I realized at that moment that I definitely was not my mind, because my mind would not listen to me and stop thinking so I could get to sleep."

Marty got it. Marty got it at the deepest level. He truly understood that he was not his mind. This is such an important distinction for you as a coach. When you begin to recognize that what you are thinking, feeling and experiencing at the body level is not who you are, but something that is happening to you, then you can move to a place where you are no longer being controlled by what you are feeling, thinking, or experiencing. *You* are in control.

The Dreaded Mixed Message

The body, mind and feelings are all channels of communication. When someone is speaking to us and their words don't match their body language or the feelings they are expressing, or the feelings they are generating in us, we say they are sending a mixed message. If they say "Look, I'm fine with what you said in the meeting," but the tone is aggressive, that's a mixed message. The mind is being told everything is okay, but the feelings aren't getting the same message.

Obviously it's important in your role as a developer of people not to send mixed messages. If your body language and tone of voice don't match the message you are sending verbally, the effect will be negative and your credibility will be compromised. It is equally important not to send such messages to *yourself*. It's hard to maintain confidence, for example, when your mind is saying, "I can do this," but your body posture, closely resembling the letter C, is telling you, "Not a chance."

If you don't make an effort to notice what you're experiencing, however, you'll be dominated and controlled by it. Unless you have that awareness and act on it, you can be hijacked by what you are experiencing, as the following illustrates:

John, a sales executive with a medium-sized paper company in Atlanta, Georgia, was on a joint sales call with one of his top sales associates. The client had been screened and was considered a prime candidate to become a major client. John had spoken with the senior buyer at a Rotary Club meeting a week earlier, and the buyer had been keen to connect with John and the sales associate. He had given John every indication that the sale would be, in John's words, virtually a "slam dunk."

They were barely into the meeting when the senior buyer turned to John and said, "This is not what we spoke about. You're wasting our time." John was stunned. He said he tried to recover, but his feelings took over and he stumbled through his reply, cut off his sales associate and directed all his comments at the buyer. The meeting went nowhere, ended poorly, and John and the associate left 10 minutes later, stopping at a small bar to debrief the performance.

Within 10 minutes, John told me, he could think of everything he should have said and done in the meeting. It isn't that he suddenly got smarter. When we become what we are experiencing, we move into what is referred to as the "choker's profile"; arousal level goes up, the focus of attention narrows, and we miss relevant information and literally become narrow-minded. John knew what to do but he couldn't access his skills because, in the grip of his own emotions, he was reacting badly to the buyer's comment. His associate commented that the other people in the meeting had also reacted to the buyer's rudeness and were sympathetic to John, but so overpowering was his reaction that he didn't notice and eventually lost them as allies.

I asked John to tell me what he experienced at each of the three levels: body, mind and feelings. It was easy for him to recreate the scene. He said that at the body level, his face started to flush, he felt suddenly warm, his heart rate increased and his breathing was shallow and quick. At the feeling level he was experiencing a mixture of frustration, uncertainty and betrayal as well as some panic and a touch of anger. At the mind level his thoughts raced between "I can't believe this" and "I've got to calm down," but when he searched for an idea his mind seemed blank.

What John needed were self-management skills that he could apply in the moment to manage what he was experiencing internally so that he could perform externally. (The website associated with this chapter, www.ignitingthethirdfactor.com, is your mental training room to prepare for just such moments.) John needed to notice what was going on and then act on that information. He could have employed what we jokingly call the FART technique—First Ask for a Repeat of the Threat—using words such as "What aspects of what we're covering do you think are a waste of time?" This would have bought John time to calm down. He could have used a centering breathing technique to manage his arousal level. He could have changed the way he was speaking to himself, or reframed the buyer's comment as a request for information (rather than a threat) and then dealt with it in a more effective manner. The point is, there are many things you can do to get back on course, but these, like all skills, have to be practiced.

The Power of Breath

Just as self-talk can inform you about your beliefs, your breathing is a litmus test of how you are reacting to and dealing with a situation. Once you start noticing, you'll be amazed at how much your breathing reveals about your inner world, exposing what was hidden from you before. If your breathing is short, hard and shallow, you can be certain that something is impacting on you whether you're aware of what it is or not. The breath is a wise messenger—it knows all!

In many types of meditation the breath is the focal point, informing the meditator. If you are someone who experiences stress at the physical level—tight chest, headaches, sore back, tightening and rising shoulders—then breathing techniques are for you. Why do I say this? If the symptom is physical, then it only makes good sense to go in with a skill at the physical level. Other techniques might work too, but it's best to deal with physical symptoms directly, addressing the problem right where it lives—in the body.

The centering breathing technique is a powerful skill used by many Olympic and world champions and their coaches. You won't believe the difference it will make in your ability to self-manage. I use this skill more than any other to manage myself in high-pressure situations so that I can be effective in working with athletes, coaches and business leaders. (By the way, if you're a golfer, this simple technique can take strokes off your golf game!)

This centering skill is easier to learn if someone is walking you through it. If you visit the website www.ignitingthethirdfactor.com, I will be your guide.

When you do notice what is happening—frustration, increased heart rate, anger, negative self-talk—you can begin to self-manage by using learned skills to reduce, transform or eliminate the feelings, thoughts or body symptoms you are experiencing. Some skills are designed to help you adjust or modify your perspective (e.g., reframing or self-talk). Others are from the area of energy management (e.g., the centering breathing technique). Or we might use imagery to circumvent what we are experiencing. The point is, when we notice that something isn't as it should be, we have choices about how to deal with it.

You Observing "You"

The first step in becoming actively aware is called *disidentification*, a term first coined by the Italian psychiatrist Roberto Assagioli. It refers to the capacity to step back and notice what is happening from the position of the Self, also known as the neutral observer or Fair Witness. This is critical in determining what is *really* happening. Somebody once said, "I don't know who discovered water but I'm sure it wasn't fish." When you are in the middle of something, especially if that something is really important to you, it's difficult to form an accurate picture of what is happening and then determine what needs to happen. You need to separate yourself and your desires, beliefs and expectations from the mix and see reality.

The coaches I interviewed all have a tremendous capacity to step back at critical moments and see what needs to happen. They do this in evaluating performances, in evaluating themselves and their actions, and in evaluating new ideas or possibilities for their teams and athletes. This is not only about managing moment-to-moment situations but also about being able to see what is needed in the long term rather than getting caught up in tunnel vision due to, for example, past success ("I've always done it this way").

We will see later that this ability to disengage, disidentify and in an unbiased manner determine what is happening and what needs to happen is especially critical when a performer is blocked or dealing with adversity. Here we talk about being able to do this for yourself.

There are three steps in active awareness: disidentify, choose, and act. Notice what is going on, make a choice, and then act to support that choice. The actions are the psychological skills—reframing, self-talk, affirmation, centering (breathing techniques), imagery, and others—that are found in any good book on performance psychology. We include a short example at the end of this chapter, but by accessing the website associated with this book you can get information on all of these techniques and, in some instances, I'll guide you through the step-by-step process of acquiring the skill.

Let's return to our meeting example. An advantage of the meeting environment is that we can quite easily disengage and disidentify every so often and see what's happening to us as a result of what is transpiring or has already transpired. These small gaps allow us to become aware and to make sure we are on our intended course, that we have not been hijacked by strong feelings, intense thoughts or the stories we have made up about what has taken place.

The next time you're in a meeting, try this: Push your chair back slightly from the table, look inside yourself and see what you find. Scan your body, checking for tension in your vulnerable spots. Mine are the jaw muscles, neck, chest and back. Notice what you are thinking and decide if it's helpful. Is it supporting you and helping you achieve the state you decided you wanted to be in, where you display your best leadership? Sometimes when I do this I discover that I've brought inner "stuff" with me into the meeting from elsewhere that is affecting my performance here and now.

For many years I sat on a medical/scientific committee that, among other things, organized medical coverage and drug testing for large international events held in Canada. Our meetings took place several times a year, from 7 till 10 in the evening. The agendas were often ambitious, and there was pressure to get things done on time. I remember arriving a bit early for one meeting and chatting with the chairman, Norm Gledhill. He said to me at one point, "Peter, you're not your usual chipper self. What's going on?" I immediately dismissed his question, said I was fine and sat down, feeling a bit irritated. But then I slipped inside and quickly noticed that I was *not* fine and that I was more than a little irritated.

I thought back to dinnertime and realized I had been irritated even then, but when I retraced my day, I remembered that lunchtime had been a much different story, with a lot of fun and laughter. I asked myself, "What happened between lunch and dinner?" Through some inner detective work I was able to realize that it was a mid-afternoon phone call from someone I really didn't care for that had set me off. This person had asked me to do something in the evening meeting that I didn't think was ethical.

So let's take stock here. It was seven o'clock at night and I was still irritated by a phone call from someone I didn't respect that had occurred four hours earlier, at 3 p.m. I was giving this person way too much control over how I felt, and, as a result, over my behavior. I had to get rid of him! I was giving him attention—attention that he didn't deserve. I could have taken any number of actions. I could have used the centering breathing technique to reduce my arousal level and calm down. I could have reframed the situation or changed the way I was speaking to myself. But what I chose was to run an image: a letting-go image.

First I thought of him and what he reminded me of. That led directly to the image that would allow me to get rid of him. I won't tell you what he reminded me of, but you'll probably figure it out from my imagery. As I sat there in the meeting I imagined flushing this arrogant man down a toilet. I could see him spinning around in the bowl, his tie sticking out in Dilbert fashion, his pompous voice saying, "You can't do this to me" . . . and then he was gone! And he truly was gone. I was back to being myself and able to join in the meeting with my usual enthusiasm.

The beauty of meetings is that the opportunity to disidentify is present at many points, and absolutely no one knows you're doing it. The bonus for you and for them is that when you come back moments later, you're a much better team player.

Debbie Muir's story near the start of this chapter concerning her high heart rate at the L.A. Olympics is a great example of active awareness. So is the following one from gold medalist David Hemery, describing the last half-hour before the 400 meter hurdle race, which he won by seven meters in the Mexico City Olympics of 1968.

"I have used imagination before a race to keep the nerves under control. Before a race you would have 15 minutes with your competitors in an area about the size of a small changing room. I would lie down on a bench with my head resting on the soft side of my shoes and close my eyes and try to take my breathing down to slow my heart rate so that I was under control.

"One of the favorites started jogging, so the others also started jogging, but I thought, 'I've got time on the track, so just stay under control.' I was trying to keep mentally under control through physiological methods.

"On the warm-up track I stopped at the outside of the track, but facing the track, and was changing from jogging shoes into spikes when, out of the corner of my eye, I saw Jeff [an American runner] take a start from the blocks. The movement was so fast it caught my eye. I watched this guy go round the bend and I thought, 'Gosh he's fast,' and I could feel my heart reach into my throat and then I thought, 'I'm supposed to run faster than that?' I recognized the lack of helpfulness of that thought! I couldn't control how fast he ran.

"I immediately switched my thoughts to 'When did you feel the best you could, running with power and control and feeling great?' I thought about coming back from a hamstring tear the year before and going to the beach at Duxbury on the coast in Massachusetts. It was a long beach, with firm sand and shallow water at the edge. I had gone into about six inches of water and was running like a trotting horse. The cushioned landing wasn't hurting the hamstring, so I gradually moved up the pace until I was running at about a pace you would run a 400 meter lap. I was really moving well, and I held it for what seemed like hundreds and hundreds of meters. I couldn't believe it! And then I took it up to a full sprint and I must have gone for at least 150 meters at a full sprint, to a point when I started easing back and thinking, 'Oh my God, what a feeling!'

"So on the side of the warm-up track in Mexico City I told myself, 'Take your shoes and socks off, the infield is damp from the afternoon rain. Run on the infield for 50 or 100 meters ... take yourself back to the feeling of flow.' I did, and within 50 meters I was back on the edge of the water with the sun on my back, feeling the power of running freely. The other stuff had gone and I was just within my own power—with the best sense of well-being I could have experienced—of strength, and speed, and power, and enjoyment of movement. It set me up to be able to act on what I could control. There is nothing you can do about the opposition."

There you have it. Disidentify, notice what is happening, choose what you need to do, and act. Oh, and go out and win the gold medal!

In contrast with John's story earlier in this chapter, where his performance with the buyer was sabotaged by what he was experiencing,

David was able to step back at the critical moment, disidentify and regain his gold-medal confidence.

Cut Yourself Some Slack

Too many people use verbal lashings to motivate themselves. Not only is this unproductive, ineffective and hard on the individual, but also it's unhealthy. When you take on the role of developing another person you are doing more than supervising them. You need to be as supportive of yourself as you are of them. You cannot be the heckler in the crowd of your own performance and expect to do well.

Another common mistake is to give too much respect to the task at hand, building it up to the level of pyramid construction. Figure skater Kurt Browning, in discussing a triple axel jump he was struggling with, once told me, "I'm giving that jump way too much respect." He switched to a lighter approach, and after a few minutes, nailed it.

What you are doing in your role is important, but it is not life-and-death brain surgery. When you do get down on yourself or are in a bit of a funk, stop and think about how you would motivate your best friend in the same state. If you do this it's quite likely you'll discover that you have one set of rules for motivating others and another set for yourself. Can it really be true that more than six billion people need support and optimism when they are down or facing a challenge, but you need something totally different?

Extinguishers often have a complete lack of awareness and therefore:
- They don't know and couldn't care less about how they make others feel.
- They believe they know what is "right."
- They only restrain themselves in front of "superiors."

To be an Igniter remember this!
- Understand the impact you have on others.
- Know your beliefs.
- Take conscious action to manage yourself.

Editor: Hold on here. That's a pretty heady concept, disidentification.

Author: It is, but it's one of those words that really explains itself. When you disidentify, you simply step back from what you're experiencing and move to a position of neutral observer. When we identify with what we are experiencing—fear, disappointment, insecurity—we begin to shrink and become much less than we truly are. When we disengage and observe what we are experiencing, we expand what is possible because we can access all of our abilities and skills.

Editor: I get it in the abstract, but can you give me a practical example?

Author: Sure. My wife, Sandra, went to a small resort many years ago to do a presentation to a group of recreation specialists, many of whom were her colleagues and peers. The night before the presentation she inadvertently locked herself out of her room, and because all the staff had gone home, she had to sleep, somewhat uncomfortably, on a small couch in the room of one of her friends. She finally got into her own room in the morning and was getting ready for a full day of presenting when she noticed that she was feeling "off" and her confidence was wavering.

She literally stepped back from herself and observed what was going on inside. She noticed that she was tired, anxious and a little worried about presenting to her peers. But she was also able to see that this wasn't the whole picture. Managing yourself is not about denial or pretending that everything is okay. When you disengage and disidentify, you may see that you are anxious, tired, worried or whatever else—but that's only part of the whole truth at that moment.

Sandra asked herself, "What else am I? What else is also true?" Stepping back and disidentifying enabled her to capture all of who she was at that moment. She was able to remind herself that she was also competent, well-organized, respected, a good teacher and someone with a keen sense of humor.

Psychologist and meditation expert Tara Brach says that all "dis-ease" is "home" sickness in that we need to remember who we truly are and return home—that is, back to our true self. She talks about how we shrink when we become what we are experiencing and become less than we truly are. We become a sliver of the pie rather than the whole pie.

Editor: Have you noticed that whenever you say something significant or meaningful, you tend to talk about an experience your wife has had? That really clears it up for me.

Author: (Fails to respond due to self-induced brain lock.)

4

Build Trust

Editor: There can be no debate about the importance of trust in any relationship, particularly one where developing another person is the central concern. But trust is one of those words that (trust me!) gets a lot of lip service without much thought for its true meaning. There are actually many types of trust, aren't there?

Author: There are indeed. We may trust someone—an airline pilot, for example—simply because of his qualifications. This may also be true of professionals such as doctors, police or firefighters, but media revelations have had the effect of diluting that trust to some degree in Western societies. Increasingly, it seems to me, our trust is on a shorter and shorter leash.

Editor: I would agree that in the current climate we are less likely to put our trust in someone than we used to—at least initially. So are we going to focus on the building of trust between two people in a relationship where one is trying to develop the other?

Author: Yes, because without trust and a sense of safety and security, it's impossible to create an environment that encourages the full disclosure and engagement necessary for developing another person. The Third Factor grows best in an environment of trust. Coaches and leaders who have a strong developmental bias really get this, and one of the first things they do is build a trusting relationship with the other person.

Editor: Well, just for the record I'm going to let my guard down, and for the moment, trust that you know what you're doing, at least in terms of what needs to be covered in this chapter. Please don't screw it up. I need this book to succeed.

Author: Ahh . . . unconditional trust if I've ever heard it!

BUILD TRUST

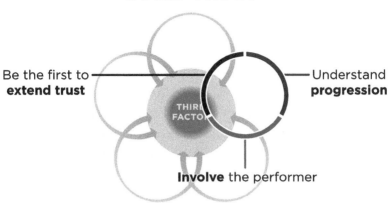

Be the first to **extend trust** —————————— **Understand progression**

THIRD FACTOR

Involve the performer

G arry Watanabe, one of our corporate trainers, told me a story about a facilities manager in a Toronto-area municipality. It had come to light that a certain mechanic was available to fill a vacant position. The downside was that this otherwise qualified person had a bad reputation as a malcontent and troublemaker. The manager remembered sitting in on the interview when this person was hired by the city and being impressed by the individual's desire to make a positive impact on families and communities.

Because he had an opening, and partly out of curiosity, the manager considered bringing this person over. But when he thought about what it would take to make it work, he realized it was not up to just him, so he called a meeting of his team. He told them what he was thinking of doing and why, and asked the team if they felt they would be able to create the kind of environment where people have a fair opportunity to redeem themselves. He said the decision to bring the person on would have to be unanimous, and he allowed them to decide via anonymous ballot.

With the team in agreement, the manager brought the individual on board. He realized he needed to set a tone of honesty with this person right off the bat, so in his first conversation he acknowledged the negative rumors but let him know he would have a chance to prove himself based upon his performance and his ability to get along with the other facility workers. He gave the individual his cell number and said that he believed in his ability to get the job done, but that he was also aware that occasionally "questions would arise" that he might need help with. He told the individual that if he ever found himself needing information he was not able to get easily from a co-worker or his supervisor, he was to use the number. The manager also made it clear that if he was ever in doubt as to whether to use the number or not, he was expected to call.

Within a few months, the reviews from co-workers were unanimously positive: the new employee was quiet and not easy to get to know, but he was a skilled, dedicated worker who was not afraid of hard work and was eager to help out his teammates.

This manager demonstrated the sort of building of trust that is of paramount importance at the start or restart of a relationship. He also demonstrated trust in his entire work group.

I don't need to build a case for the necessity of trust between coach and trainee. Would you want someone you didn't trust to be your mentor? How open would you be with this person in describing the fears and feelings that were getting in the way of your moving to the next level? How much would you even trust them to have your best interests at heart? Right . . . about as much as you'd trust Jack the Ripper with your new Cutco knives!

Clearly, you won't succeed in igniting the Third Factor in a performer unless and until that person feels assured that you are in their corner—you're *there* for them. They can be sure that their trust in you isn't misplaced. Without trust, you won't get to first base developmentally. Your role will be vastly diminished, from the high ground of a developer of people to, at best, a supervisor, a checker who makes sure things are being done right and corners aren't being cut. Which means much less opportunity to build a meaningful connection with that person, and a mutual sense of purpose. Build trust and wonderful things are possible—for both of you.

There are other reasons, performance reasons, why trust is so important. Simply put, **trust leads to commitment, and committed people**

outperform others. Olympic coaches understand that exceptional performance occurs only in a safe environment where athletes can develop self-awareness and confidence.

In his book *The Five Dysfunctions of a Team,* Patrick Lencioni points out that without trust, one cannot confront key issues required to turn an organization or team around. To deal with difficult and challenging issues, people need to know they are safe. They need to know that they can trust their leader and their team members.

Of course this is also true at the individual level. When someone is blocked or not moving forward, the obstacle that's in the way often must be confronted. Confronting is much more effective when trust is present. In one of our leadership programs at Queen's University, a manager in the pharmaceutical industry talked about conducting a touchy performance appraisal with a technically strong performer. In the formal review, she indicated to the employee that technically, her performance had been above standard in every category, and that this had also been the case the previous year. She then put away all her notes and said to the employee, "That's my formal appraisal. Now, would you like my informal one so you can understand what's holding you back?"

When the employee agreed, she proceeded to outline with precision the interpersonal behaviors with teammates that were holding her back from reaching the next level. A year earlier, the manager told me, this conversation could not have taken place; she didn't yet have a relationship built on trust with this particular employee. She had spent the year developing rapport and a sense of trust with this individual and was now able to give her the feedback she needed to move forward.

When trust is present, people being asked to do something exceedingly difficult or challenging or risky, in an environment of continuous or rapid change, exhibit a much greater reach. When Olympic coaches expose their athletes to high-risk elements, the athletes must trust that the coach knows what they are capable of and will not put them in situations where they will fail.

This is equally true in the non-athletic world. When people embark on risky moves or deal with rapid change, for example, they're often, to quote my wife, Sandra Stark, "between trapezes." In such circumstances you need a safety net, and that safety net is trust—in the coach, manager, parents or other team members.

We sometimes naïvely think that trust is about being nice and well-liked, but you will not be trusted if you are not perceived as being *competent*. Your employees' trust in you as their coach will be connected to their perception of you as a competent leader secure in your abilities. This is one of the reasons developmental coaches are lifetime learners. They never cease trying to get better, to expand their knowledge, and to fine-tune their repertoire of techniques and skills. Mel Davidson, coach of Canada's gold-medal-winning women's Olympic hockey team, says, "It's important that the players perceive you striving to be better and learn at a higher level. I feel a lot of time we as coaches get caught up in the coaching world (in sport) and forget about what we can learn outside of it, whether it's professional development or hanging out with somebody else." Do your people see you trying to improve your own performance?

Stephen M.R. Covey, author of *The SPEED of Trust,* points out that when there's a decrease in trust, there's an increase in cost and time. He cites 9/11 and airport security as an example. This is certainly true at the office/team level as well. If people are uncertain about whether they trust their teammates or colleagues, things take a lot longer to move forward and people are less open, less disclosing and less willing to share.

What Can You Do to Develop Trust?

Before we dive into the three key ways that you develop trust, I want to make a point concerning the deliberateness with which coaches with a strong developmental bias approach the building of trust. The coaches I interviewed and those I have observed over the years don't assume that trust will occur automatically, even for a team that has been together for a long time. Coaches are very intentional in their development of trust. They build it through precise, clear communication of a repetitive nature related to drills, skill development, performance goals, end goals, values and vision. Coaches are the first to extend trust, they understand progression, and they involve the performer.

Be the First to Extend Trust

"The only way to make a man trustworthy is to trust him." — Henry Stimson

Trust is a two-way street. In order to receive it, you first must give it. The more of it you give away, the more you will get in return. It can be extended in the simple act of tossing the keys of your car to your young son, or in the more complex commitment of standing by performers when they are having difficulty, or even when they fail.

Several years ago I spent some time watching figure skating coach Doug Leigh working with a 17-year-old senior-level skater. She had gone home for the summer as a young girl and returned in September as a woman. Her whole body had changed. Her new physical dimensions and the change in her center of mass were causing her great difficulty with jumps that she had mastered easily in the spring. In the 15 minutes I watched her practice, she had many, many falls and was getting thoroughly frustrated. Doug called her over, looked her in the eye, and, pointing to his feet, said, "You see these feet? They aren't going anywhere. You are working hard, you're pushing yourself—you're doing everything you can."

What a marvelous way to communicate the reassurance that you understand someone's struggle and that you're solidly there for them. It's this kind of presence and reassurance that builds trust. It confirms that you can be relied on; that you're not going to bail at the first sign of difficulty.

"To gain trust, you have to be trustworthy," says coach David Hemery, stressing that it's important for a coach to be consistent—"walking the walk; saying what you mean and meaning what you say." Over time, as this pattern of behavior is continually reinforced, trust develops. "A lot of people talk a good game and then act differently," he says. "That would lose my trust if I were an athlete."

He also believes it's important for the performer to be able to take the coach's intent into account, so that even in situations where there might be some question or even doubt in the performer's mind about the methods being used, there's none about the coach's integrity and intentions. "If you trust that the coach is not trying to exploit you or manipulate you for his own glory, then it's more likely you'll give more," he says.

Being in the senior position, it's up to the coach, parent or leader to initiate the building of trust. It can't be left to occur by accident. Good coaches consciously work on developing trust, within the team and between the team and the coaching staff.

Prior to the 2006 Olympics in Torino, hockey coach Mel Davidson designed a month-long training camp on Prince Edward Island. The sole purpose was to build trust between the players as well as with the coaching staff. She considered it a vital first step. Over the course of the month, players were placed in various groups in cabins and tents. She told me that sometimes players would come to her and tell her things were not going so well in their small group. Often it amounted to disagreements over trivial matters. She would listen to the complaints and then send the athletes back to work it out with their colleagues, trusting them to do that and to learn to rely on each other. When she speaks of the Torino Olympics in corporate seminars or public presentations, that month of trust building is what she focuses on. To her it was the foundation of all future success.

Synchronized swimming coach Debbie Muir also spoke with me about the importance of trust in her team. Here's some of what she had to say:

> "When I look back I can see ways that I built trust through the years. I think intuitively I knew that had to happen, and that the best way to build trust is through role modeling. You become reliable. You are role modeling how you want *them* to be. When you let them know you, they start to trust you, so I always tried to model all the values and things I was trying to get them to do. Honesty was one, and often I was the first to extend it. I would say, 'I'm really nervous, how about you?'"

It's important to demonstrate honesty by *being* honest, she says, so that athletes know beyond any doubt that you are not going to lie to them. It's the only way to build trust.

If you stop and think for a moment about people you trust and why you trust them, you will get some ideas as to what you can do to build trust in your team or work group. Once you identify those behaviors that you want to encourage and reinforce, you need to take the initiative and act on them. This act of taking the initiative—of being the first to extend trust—is the first step in developing trust in those in your care.

Below is a questionnaire we use in our team workshop on developing trust. Take a moment to fill it out before you read on.

Building Trust Self-Assessment

Demonstrating your trust in others builds their trust in you. How well do you demonstrate your trust in others? Complete this self-assessment using the following scale:

1	2	3	4	5
Never	Seldom	Sometimes	Often	Always

I admit my mistakes.

| 1 | 2 | 3 | 4 | 5 |

I listen to other people and their ideas.

| 1 | 2 | 3 | 4 | 5 |

I think about what I am going to say and how I am going to say it.

| 1 | 2 | 3 | 4 | 5 |

I keep my team/people informed by sharing information, thoughts and feelings.

| 1 | 2 | 3 | 4 | 5 |

I tell the truth.

| 1 | 2 | 3 | 4 | 5 |

I don't allow put-downs of others.

| 1 | 2 | 3 | 4 | 5 |

I am predictable. My team/people know what I stand for, value and support.

| 1 | 2 | 3 | 4 | 5 |

I honor my commitments. (I do what I say I will do.)

| 1 | 2 | 3 | 4 | 5 |

I raise difficult issues.

| 1 | 2 | 3 | 4 | 5 |

I communicate to others that I appreciate their skills, abilities and resources.

| 1 | 2 | 3 | 4 | 5 |

My behavior is consistent with my intentions.

| 1 | 2 | 3 | 4 | 5 |

I encourage all team members to participate.

| 1 | 2 | 3 | 4 | 5 |

I avoid talking about others when they are not present.

| 1 | 2 | 3 | 4 | 5 |

I take others at face value.

| 1 | 2 | 3 | 4 | 5 |

In our workshops we have another simple self-assessment exercise, "Establishing Rapport and Respect." You can find the entire questionnaire on the website. The format uses numbers 1 to 5 (1= Never; 3 = Sometimes; 5 = Always) to indicate the degree to which the statements in each question represent the respondent's behavior or actions.

My wife, Sandra, a counselor, along with our colleague Peggy, developed the questionnaire, and I remember being one of the first to be asked to fill it out. When I'd completed it, thinking they wanted feedback I commented that they had really taken the concepts of respect and rapport and fleshed them out nicely to include actions that people could perform to improve in those areas. Sandra asked me how I'd done on question six: "I make it easy for people to tell me they don't know something."

That immediately made me suspicious. My wife refers to me on occasion as a flaming optimist, so even though I had rated myself a 5 on the item, I downgraded it to a 4 (being an optimist, however, I couldn't help adding, "but I might be a 5!").

Sandra then informed me that Peggy had done an assessment of me with reference to the questionnaire and rated me a 2 on that question. She thought Peggy had been generous. "I, on the other hand, who know you much better, rated you a 1 because there is no zero on the scale."

I was incredulous. "How could you do that?" I demanded.

Her response was a shock to me—but very revealing. She told me that my body language and tone of voice conveyed a highhandedness and dismissiveness that were completely off-putting. "You think you're being funny when you say things like 'I can't believe you don't know that. Everybody knows that. Didn't they teach you anything at university?' We don't want to hear that," she said. "We just want the answer to our question, so often we will go elsewhere or take the time to figure it out ourselves."

Difficult as this was to hear, it was great feedback. It was an unequivocal reminder that in order to build trust in others, you need a healthy dose of self-awareness, and one of the best ways to acquire this is to ask those in your charge how they view you. That will soon put you in tune with how effective you're being! Synchronized swimming coach Debbie

Muir made that point very well in our interview. She said that at a certain point she started to notice how she was acting at competitions and realized that her behavior might not be proving all that useful for her athletes, whom she really trusted. So she put it to them: "Okay, how can I be most effective? How do I make you crazy at meets?" The result was honest and open dialogue on both sides, which benefited both her and the athletes.

Let's go back to our meeting as a model for applying the concepts we've been discussing. There are three Cs related to extending trust: Caring, Consistency, and Competence. When you filled out the questionnaire a few pages back, how did you fare? Meetings are a great place to show people that you have trust in them. Leaders with a developmental bias will be more facilitative in their meeting style, allowing others to take the lead and, at times, ownership of key issues and their resolution. Building a trusting environment where people feel safe to speak their truth all starts with you and how you manage any impulse to react when you may not agree or may consider their thinking naïve. Progression is very important in this regard.

Understand Progression

Because self-esteem is critical, "progression" too is critical. **Your performers need to know** that you, as their coach or leader, truly understand their current level of performance, and **that you're fully aware of their level of competence.** This requires you to be knowledgeable enough in your field to have a clear picture of the progression, or continuum, of their development. A gymnastics coach, for example, does not start by teaching a front handspring, but begins with a simpler skill such as a front somersault. A good coach doesn't hesitate to say when an athlete is not yet ready for a particular progression, even though that person may appear to possess the physical skills. Only gradually will the coach introduce the performer to that level, to build confidence and ensure ultimate success. Eventually the athlete will have developed the ability to compete at the higher level.

Now this might appear, at first glance, to be a contradiction of what I said earlier on how inner turmoil, disappointment and dissatisfaction are necessary to create the energy needed by the Third Factor to move forward. These things are the "match" that often ignites the Third Factor, creating the inevitable force that ensures change. Clearly, the igniting of the Third Factor can't take place in environments that are overprotective; there needs to be some risk and challenge involved.

I've also talked about creating a safe environment and the need for progression and the avoidance of absolute failure—and yet there is also the need for risk and some uncertainty to help people improve their performance. I think of it as being like physical exercise. Too little stress produces little or no benefit, whereas too much can lead to overuse injuries and other long-term problems. The right level of stress—of challenge—is what is needed. You, the leader, really need to know your people and their capabilities and, most important, their level of confidence with a particular task. Confidence is very task-specific. In my case, for example, I am a confident public speaker but not at all confident singing karaoke.

As developers of people, we need to be forward-looking—to be able to visualize how the other person will process the outcome of their actions. To what will they attribute success or failure? Will it be to something over which they have control and can develop, or will it be something outside their control, such as circumstance? In most situations you would like the performer to attribute success to something they did—or, in the case of a poor performance, to something they *should have done* or *could do* to prepare for the next performance.

Good coaches do not put their performers in a position where they are going to fail. Again, that may seem contradictory to one of our main tenets: embrace adversity. But, while recognizing that there's a fine line, good coaches do not allow their young athletes, especially early on in their development, to experience a devastating failure. There will be mistakes—and lots of them—but they will be dealt with as lessons. Confidence—real confidence, not bravado—is hard to come by, so it's important not to jeopardize it.

Progression and learning are inexorably linked. The developer's role is to reinforce that link in the mind of a performer. The learner needs to understand and experience the connection between following a clear progression and being successful, whether it's learning to use a computer program or completing a triple jump in figure skating.

And as a coach you need to know your people well in order to be able to adapt a path to fit each individual, their skill level, and perhaps most important, their level of confidence. A proper plan of progression helps ensure the building of confidence, which often leads the performer to greater reach—and exceptional performance.

Good coaches also understand that they may not be the perfect fit for every one of their performers in all aspects of their training. A coach who has always had a high level of confidence may not be able to relate to a performer who, though technically competent, doesn't often display that competence because of a lack of confidence. And the performer, sensing the disconnect around this issue, may not really trust the coach. A perceptive coach will see that what is needed here is a mentor, someone who has "been there," who has overcome low confidence. The very act of admitting you are not the best person to handle a particular situation and referring the performer to someone better suited can have a powerful impact. It can be a significant step in the building of trust.

In summary, progression involves planning and modifying a developmental path to suit the needs of each performer. Understand that it is the whole person who performs, and that while a person may appear to be ready at one level, they may not be at another. Getting them "game ready" involves working on all the skills in the continuum.

What's Regression?

Several years ago at a workshop at Queen's University, a participant who was a manager at a large medical supply company told me about a young woman she had hired who had graduated in the sciences with excellent marks. In just six months, this young woman had rocketed into the top 20 percent of the company's sales producers, chiefly by overcoming some of the barriers orthopedic surgeons commonly employed to "protect" themselves from salespeople. A most impressive track record, given her age and inexperience.

On the strength of her performance, someone higher in the organization than her manager decided that the young star should be sent in to tackle their most difficult challenge: a senior U.S.-based orthopedic surgeon whose behavior they described as "abusive." This man, in his 70s and from the era of "doctor as God," directed a large hip-replacement clinic the company had so far been unable to penetrate.

The result of the sales meeting? He chewed her up and spat her out. She was devastated.

The manager's comment was telling: "That happened months ago," she said, "and we still haven't got her back to where she was when we hired her." And unhappily, without proper coaching they may *never* get her back to where she was—but worse, she may never reach her potential.

There are several troubling aspects to this story, not the least being the impact on the young woman and her self-esteem. It turns out that there was no real coaching available to prepare her mentally for a challenge that was so much more difficult than anything she had previously faced in her budding career.

I also learned that they had not sent anyone in with her, so there was no proper way to debrief her performance and ensure that her lack of success was attributed not to her, but to the doctor. If, as soon as possible after the sales call, there had been a debriefing with someone who witnessed what took place, perhaps this young woman could have been spared the upset she experienced. Someone who saw and heard what was said could have pointed out to her, for example, that her opening was exactly the one that had been so successful with many other doctors, and that the reason it wasn't with him had to do with him, not with her approach. Without proper debriefing there was no way to effectively diminish the impact he had on her. (She needed to be told that this doctor was a man who certainly would never develop hemorrhoids because he was a perfect asshole!)

In summary, this young woman was sent in far too early in her learning curve to deal with such a difficult person. There was no witness to what took place. The company was no further ahead with this particular client, and one of their top salespeople was no longer performing at a high level. But by far the worst outcome was that the whole enterprise resulted in devastation, not development, for the young woman.

Focus on Performance Goals to Achieve Exceptional End Goals

Progression is also about reach: What is this person capable of at this moment? How far should they be stretched so they can develop and build the self-confidence to take them even further, and not be hobbled in the attempt? Often the best way to determine the reach of another person is simply to ask them. Or let them show you by way of how they handle an open challenge, one in which they demonstrate their capability.

Part of progression, for elite coaches, is to focus on performance goals, not end goals; to keep the performer's attention focused on what they need to do in the moment, not what they want to achieve ultimately. John Wooden rarely, if ever, mentioned winning. He did not overload his athletes with the burden of the end goal but instead had them focus on the steps that would help them achieve that goal. This is a vital point. The press and public sometimes get upset with athletes or performers who decline to state publicly that they will win the gold medal, the World Series or the Stanley Cup. There is a common belief that this is somehow connected to the performer's weakness, fear or lack of will. Nothing could be further from the truth.

Think of performance goals as the steps in a staircase and the end goal as the final landing at the top flight of stairs. The goal of the coach, manager or teacher is to keep the focus of the performer on their current step. But in the workplace, for example, it is not uncommon for people to be badgered about where they are in relation to quarterly or year-end results, in the belief that this will motivate them to achieve the desired outcome. In reality, it simply overloads them and robs them of some of their focus.

Hammering people over the head with the end goal leads to even more devastating results when the gap between current performance and end goal widens. Competition is a motivating force only when you feel you have a chance to succeed. You only have to watch children at play to grasp this concept. The minute the game they are playing gets one-sided, half the children—those on the losing side—make noises that they are about to quit. Fortunately, children usually have the wisdom to reselect the teams or modify the game to keep everybody motivated and interested.

Involve the Performer

As a developer of others, ultimately your job is to put yourself out of work, or at least dramatically reduce the need for your services. In developing trust with others, it's crucial to involve them extensively in their own development. In the sporting world, coaches with a strong developmental bias know that as a performer matures, there is a dramatic shift from their input to the performer's own. This shift occurs not only because of the coach's desire to develop an independent, freestanding performer but also because they recognize that there is more wisdom in two people than in one. Put simply, **it means making the most out of what you both know**.

This section concerns itself with engaging with the performer, and once again, those with a well-honed developmental bias will be very good at two skills we introduced in Chapter 2: asking effective questions, and engaging in active listening.

From years of working with executives and managers, not only in executive development programs at Queen's but also within organizations, I have seen numerous examples of employees' ideas and input being highly valued. I have witnessed first-hand not only the trust that develops as a result but also the increased commitment among employees. Where people are highly engaged, trust increases, and so does commitment. One of my favorite expressions is "People do not save up well for other people's holidays." If you were not involved in the process, you're not likely to have a high level of commitment or trust.

Coach Gary Winckler told me about how he decides on workouts for his performers. Through the use of key questions and observations he carefully monitors each athlete as they come to practice. How energized are they? Have they had a late night due to an exam? I asked him if this helps him decide whether he's going to use plan A, plan B, or plan C.

"Exactly. And that is fundamental to building trust. When you make the right decisions about what plan to follow and the athlete realizes later, yes, that was the best plan to use today, then they really start to gain confidence in you, and . . . when I know an athlete has confidence in me, I feel even more responsible. It's like now I have a *really* big responsibility to make sure I make the right decisions, and that makes me a better coach. It makes me think doubly about what I'm going to do tomorrow because I don't want to lose that trust."

A Sense of Ownership

There are many areas in which we can start to involve performers, extend their influence and increase their sense of ownership. Planning, problem-solving and innovation are three. One of the organizations I have the pleasure of working with allows its employees to be involved in selecting equipment they use in their jobs. Workers who drive pickup trucks, for example, test-drove four different trucks pre-selected by the company engineers, and chose the model they felt best about. The man who owned the company told me that maintenance costs for the vehicles declined 40 percent as a direct result of involving performers in the selection process.

At about the same time, I was working with front-line supervisors in a large steel company. Maintenance costs for the large trucks that moved the steel from furnaces to yard had risen astronomically due, in no small part, to employee sabotage. It turned out that the workers hated the trucks because they were slow, cumbersome and difficult to maneuver. The trucks had been designed by head-office engineers who rarely, if ever, spent time observing how they were used. They had put together a truck that featured, in their opinion, the best power train, best transmission, best chassis. No savings here! No trust or commitment either.

People want to feel valued and to know that their talents and skills are being put to good use. Quite frankly, if the people actually doing the job can't come up with better, more efficient ways of doing it, then who can? When Roger Enrico was hired as CEO of Pepsi Co., he said he was going to spend 50 percent of his time coaching his four vice-presidents, and then get them to do that with *their* reports, and so on down the line. He figured that at best, people were using 30 to 40 percent of their capabilities in the workplace and then going home and using many of their other capabilities to coach soccer, lead a Girl Guides troop, or raise money for the United Way. It is often in learning what people do outside the work world that we begin to understand their real reach and what they are capable of.

When you look back over your employment history, is there a correlation between how involved you felt and your level of trust? Where might you begin now to involve the people who report to you? Are there areas where you could extend their influence or give them a say?

I think business meetings are the perfect starting point for building trust and involving the performer. Progression reminds us that we need to know the level of competence and confidence of each performer and not put them in places where they might fail and embarrass themselves. Taking a little time before the meeting to review—not micromanage—to ensure the performer is ready is time well spent for both of you. Your developmental intentions will be clear in your words and actions, and your intent will likely be well received, building trust. Once you see they've "got it," back off and give them the forum to shine in. In meetings everyone present witnesses this extension of trust. And with trust comes reach and better results for all.

Extinguishers are not trust "worthy" because:

- They don't extend trust and only really trust themselves.
- They have not thought of, and couldn't care less about, where their people are developmentally.
- They give people work—not responsibility—and therefore don't involve people in any meaningful way.

To be an Igniter remember this!

- Be the first to extend trust. The Third Factor will emerge sooner, more frequently and with more vigor in a safe environment.
- Understand progression. Let your people know that you know where they are "at" developmentally, and that you have an understanding of the next steps.
- Involve the performer. Make the most out of what you both know.

Editor: Now that was interesting, particularly the section on progression. I hadn't really thought of that before.

I realize, in looking back to my university days and to when I first got involved in the book business, that I had some very good teachers and managers with a clear sense of progression. This will surprise you, but I have a fair level of defensiveness, so new environments were difficult for me. My first manager was great at extending trust and therefore put me at ease. This was critical for my development because I really wasn't going to learn anything until I had some level of security. It's like Maslow's hierarchy of needs. You need to take care of the basic needs before people will be interested in the high-level ones.

The manager I'm speaking of would usually meet with me in my office, where I felt more comfortable. He asked me how I like to receive my work: one project at a time or in a bundle of many projects at once. He also talked to me about when he first came on board and how uncomfortable he was. He extended trust in many ways.

Author: Those are excellent examples, and I'm glad you had such a good experience early on. What impact did it have on your performance?

Editor: Oh, I'd have gone through a wall for him. Because we both trusted each other there was really no downtime wasted on uncertainty or wondering. We worked incredibly efficiently together. It was a very sad day for me when he left. My next manager was okay, but she was uncertain of herself and tended to micromanage me too much. We spent too much time on performance and not enough on process.

Author: That last sentence is very interesting. The first manager spent a fair amount of time on process, extending trust up front that secured your exceptional performance down the line. Isn't it interesting that all the so-called soft skills are the ones that lead to hard results.

Editor: They do indeed . . . and I'm not nearly as defensive initially as I used to be.

Author: That's a blessing.

5

Encourage and Use Imagery

"Imagination is more important than knowledge." — Albert Einstein

Author: Now we're getting into the meat of it—imagery!

Editor: The meat of it? We just left a very solid chapter on trust, and now we are moving into something from fantasyland? I hope this isn't going to be "You'll see it when you believe it" or "You'll believe it when you see it," or however that goes.

Author: Oh ye of little faith! First and foremost, this is—or at least it will be for many readers— the most practical and important section in the book. Not because of anything particularly intellectual, but because once leaders truly understand imagery at the conceptual level, they change forever how they communicate with others.

Editor: Okay, you have my attention, but now back it up. I'm pleased to hear that you're not going to get intellectual because, with all due respect, I'm not sure it's your strong suit. I'm not saying that's a bad thing; it's just that I've been skeptical about the title and the content so far, and yet you really have helped me see just how practical and important that content is. I really can't imagine how imagery will be so valuable to the coach/manager. I certainly can't see myself using it to a large degree.

Author: This is too easy. Those last two sentences prove my point: "I really can't imagine . . ." "I certainly can't see . . ." You're absolutely right—you won't be able to use imagery to any effective degree.

Editor: Earth to Jensen. What was that about? I disprove your point and then you agree with me and say I made your point?

Author: Sorry, it's not my intention to confuse you. I was simply pointing out that because you could not imagine something—in this case using imagery—you aren't able to do it. People cannot do things they can't imagine. We will see as we go through this chapter that imagery is truly the language of action, of the body. We all run images all the time but just aren't aware of it—and many of them restrict us in dramatic ways. You know how we always say that over 70 percent of communication is nonverbal? That's absolutely correct. Body language is just a representation of the images that the person is running in their mind. In the chapter on trust we talked about progression, and progression is vital here as well. Let's take the time to slowly build this section so that at the end of it everyone, including you, will be able to imagine many ways they could use the language of imagery to ignite the Third Factor in those under their care.

Editor: To be honest I am intrigued, but I reserve the right to challenge imagery's practicality at the end of this chapter.

Author: Fair enough. An open mind is all any teacher can ask for.

ENCOURAGE AND USE IMAGERY

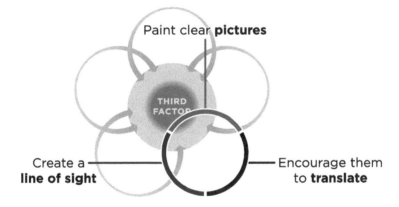

When speaking to corporate audiences I emphasize the importance of imagery in leading others. There are several reasons for this. One: it's the single most important communication skill that leaders possess. Two: because it's not something most leaders have consciously worked on and developed, there is much to gain—a huge upside for the leader. Three: it's at the foundation of every behavior. When she was conducting workshops for figure skaters and their coaches several years ago, my wife, Sandra, took some of the ideas on the power of imagery in Margo Adair's amazing book *Working Inside Out,* and blended Margo's thoughts with her own.

"Images are the language of movement. Moving in space is a right-brain activity. Images are the language of the right brain. The part of you that talks about it is not the part that can do it. Words are useful if they are translated into symbols, feelings and metaphors. Images are what instruct the body. Talk to yourself in words if you want to, but be sure that words are translated into images or feelings."

Imagery and the Third Factor

Imagery plays a key role in igniting the Third Factor within the performer. For those people with a strong imagination, who tend to think and see in pictures, imagery is the key trigger in moving them from what is to what ought to be. They can clearly "see" where they ought to be, and related images exert a strong pull on them. This will be especially true if, in addition, they tend to feel things deeply. This can cause them to become unhappy, depressed or anxious about the gap between where they see themselves in some field of endeavor and their clear picture of where they think they *should* be and what they need to be doing to get there. But at the same time, these strong feelings contribute to their activating their Third Factor.

Right off the top we need to understand that imagery fills the gap between theory—knowing about something—and performing—actually being able to do it. Imagery is the language of performance, for both the coach and the person being coached. The body doesn't speak English. It speaks Imagery!

Through this language of imagery we move theory into action. **Good coaches make constant reference to what they would "see" and "hear" in optimum situations.** For example, a coach using imagery to help someone become a caring leader might ask, "What would I *see* you doing, and what would I *hear* you saying, if you were demonstrating the qualities of a caring leader?" In answering those questions an up-and-coming leader could start the process of identifying the behaviors that, if developed, would lead to the desired goal. We cover this in more detail later.

I had a good many managers over the years who could speak eloquently and philosophically about good leadership. They could go on and on about respect and dignity, the need to involve the performer— all the things they believed a good leader or manager or parent ought to do. Yet, in practice, especially when under pressure, they did none of these things. One manager, for example, who was always talking about respect and dignity, would chew his people out in front of others when harried or under deadline pressure. The concepts of good leadership were just that, concepts. He wouldn't have known what the day-to-day applications of respect and dignity looked like if he'd tripped over them. He couldn't "see" what they looked like in action.

When we use the word *see* in this context we are including all the senses, because imagery doesn't necessarily involve seeing pictures (which is why we use the term *imagery* rather than *visualization*). For example, when learning to play golf, how a swing *feels* may be more important than how it *looks*. The workplace is no different. Helping someone become a more effective presenter at weekly meetings may work best if the person experiences through imagery what it *feels* like to stand at the front of the room and answer tough questions, rather than what it *looks* like. But most likely, more than one sense will be involved in any performance imagery.

We all have our way of combining the senses when we imagine. For many, sight is the dominant sense, but for some the sense of touch or hearing will be strongest; for others perhaps the sense of one's own body moving (kinesthesia). Toward the end of this chapter are short imagery exercises for each of the senses. Try them out and see which senses are strongest for you. The website at ignitingthethirdfactor.com has a number of expanded exercises to help you hone your imagery skills.

Imagery controls the timing and sequence of all our patterns of movement. Every action is preceded by an image. We all have the capacity for imagery, though most of the time we're unconscious of the images we're running. Aware people, when feeling down or a bit "off," for example, notice within themselves negative or self-defeating images.

Most of us have had the experience of imagining something and noticing a measurable change in our physiology as a result. Your daughter is late coming home from school and you start imagining what might have happened to her: your heart rate, your breathing and the tension level in your body all start to change in response to your negative imaginings. If we really think about it, the only reality, at least as far as our physical body is concerned, is the inner reality. What we imagine has a direct impact on our physical body. The subconscious mind does not distinguish between a real and an imagined experience.

The potential uses for imagery are immense, limited only by the breadth and scope of your own imagination. How ironic.

Images as Events

Our bodies are continually reacting and responding to our images. Images are "events" to the body, which does not distinguish between what is imagined and what is real. So if I imagine throwing a ball, the neuromuscular pathways fire in exactly the same way as if I *were* throwing the ball.

It would be hard to overestimate the importance and potential of a clear understanding of imagery for anyone wishing to develop others. Advertisers, for example, use imagery to make their pitch. Even a radio ad is trying to get you to imagine what it might feel like to drive this car or try on that type of suit or smell a particular fragrance. You can be sure that effective advertisers don't choose the *second* most powerful language to communicate their message. Imagery taps into not only the mind but also the body and feelings of the listener. **Imagery is the most powerful way we can communicate with ourselves and with others.**

Through the use of imagery you can reach inside a person's mind and throw a switch that turns on a channel full of wonderful possibilities for them. It's a powerful way to ignite the Third Factor in someone else. But what specific steps will allow you to do that? Read on.

Paint Clear Pictures of What Is Desired

It is common for coaches to tell people what they don't want them to do, but it's often difficult for them to articulate what they *do* want. This seemingly simple concept—tell people what you want, not what you don't want—is so easy to put into words, but so hard to put into action! Remember that **people can't do things they can't imagine.** Once we understand, at the cellular rather than the intellectual level, that imagery truly is the language of performance, everything opens up for us in a different way. We begin to realize, for example, that we must communicate so that people can create clear pictures in their minds of what we want, if we are going to get them to do what we want. And when we say "communicate," we don't mean just through the words we use, though our choice of words is important. If we want our people to perform in a particular way but don't behave that way ourselves, the picture we're creating can get very blurry, no matter how clear our words may be!

Speak Like a Coach

Imagine that you're shopping for groceries. You go into the store, take out the list your partner has given you—and discover that it contains only items you're *not* to purchase: How good a shopper are you likely to be with a list that says, "Don't buy ground beef, don't buy cheese, don't buy corn"? When you go into a grocery store you need a list of what you *do* want, not what you don't. It's just as important in a leadership role to paint clear pictures of what you want. As a parent, for example, ideally you would tell your child, "Make sure the books are back on the shelves and the toys are in the basket before you come down for dinner." This communication creates a clear picture of what is expected—a short, specific "to do" instruction that's easy for the child to follow. It's a much more effective communication than "Don't leave your room in a mess when you come down for dinner."

Words like *mess* don't create a clear picture of what is expected in the mind of the performer. Furthermore, as any parent will tell you, the word *mess* creates a very different picture in the child's mind than it does in the parent's. This same difference of interpretation occurs in the workplace every day. Imagine instructing an employee to "do well" on a report. When they hand it in to you two days later they tell you how well they think they've done with it—but when you read it, the report isn't close to where it should be. Should you be surprised? How "well" did you communicate your expectations?

People cannot self-adjust their performance on the basis of an unclear communication—that is, one that does not create a picture of the desired performance in the performer's mind. The coaches I interviewed told me that they routinely spend a good deal of time figuring out precisely how they want to communicate with their athletes. Synchronized swimming coach Debbie Muir told me she used the time she spent driving to the pool to hone her communication skills so that she could create the right images in the minds of her swimmers.

I asked Debbie, "How important is imagery in your coaching?" Here's what she had to say.

"Well, it's everything. The meaning of the communication is the response you get . . . right? So you think about what kind of a response you want to get back from the athlete, then structure your words and create the imagery—usually visual—that supports your words so that you get the desired response. The more conscious you are of the words you are using and the images you are setting up, the more effective you are going to be."

In general, hardly anyone spontaneously speaks the way one needs to speak when, for example, giving effective feedback. The only people who do are your golf pro or someone teaching you something. It takes practice to get good at it. As Debbie illustrates above, good coaches take the time to think about what they are going to say and how to say it. And if their performer isn't "getting it," they have to be flexible and creative. Often, they're like detectives, looking at the process as a puzzle to figure out "How can I say this so they get it this time?" The good coaches try to come at it a different way, using lateral thinking, different imagery, varied techniques in painting the picture. They may also ask others they know who are effective at getting their message across how they would say it. A composite of approaches may be required to create just the right imagery for the performer.

Self-check

Do you take the time to think about what you're going to say and how you're going to say it? In exceptional people, whether they're teachers, leaders, coaches or parents, there is a level of discipline in how they communicate— they have taken the time to stop and think about it.

Imagery is an easy concept to understand, in part because most of us are aware that imagining is something we do a good deal of the time. When we're planning to decorate a room, organizing our tasks for the day or thinking about an upcoming vacation, we employ imagery. What we are interested in here, however, is employing this language in a highly conscious and focused way to ignite in another person a picture of what is possible or what constitutes a good performance. We therefore have to **become very good at using precise language that allows others to "see" what an excellent performance looks like.**

"I Can See Clearly Now"

One of the most frustrating exercises in our coaching workshops is called "gaining clarity." We ask the five or six people at each table to pick a concept in which they would like others to have greater clarity. Let's say, for example, that a group chooses to work on the task of coaching their people to be better team players. The workshop leader then asks the group to generate a list of the skills they would encourage and develop in those people to help them become better team players. This exercise is frustrating because we are not used to speaking with the kind of precision that allows people immediately to imagine a correct and accurate performance—we tend to fall back on generalities.

In Chapter 2 we discussed the discipline required to give effective feedback. That same discipline is required here. Initially many of the groups' suggestions are vague generalizations such as that those they are coaching need to "communicate more frequently," "be a good listener," or "have a good attitude." I remind the class that these are not effective communications because they do not tell people what they would "see" and "hear" if they were engaged in good team behaviors. I jokingly ask them how they would enjoy a golf lesson from a pro who continually instructed them to hit the ball farther or to quit slicing. Such a lesson would be unhelpful and frustrating because they wouldn't be able to see a picture or get a feeling of the swing that would help them to improve their game.

I then send the class back to the drawing board with the following instructions: Take each of your generalizations—"have a good attitude," for example—and distill it into specific behaviors you would see demonstrated by someone with a good attitude. Ask "What would you see and hear someone doing who is exhibiting a good attitude?" If the first suggestion is "They listen well to others," drill down further by asking, "And what would you see and hear someone doing who was a good listener?" If they respond, "They pay attention to others," ask once more, "And what would you see and hear that tells you that they pay attention to others?" Eventually you will get down to behaviors such as "They make eye contact with other team members." "They murmur and nod their head when others are speaking to indicate they are following along." "They summarize every so often in their own words what they have heard the other person say." These are, of course, the behaviors of someone who is actively listening (a skill covered in Chapter 2 and illustrated there with the story of Robert). At the end of this exercise the participants will have gained insight into how to coach more effectively because they have distilled general concepts down to behaviors and actions that, when communicated, allow the person being coached to imagine an excellent performance or proper behavior.

If you had to coach someone to be a better golfer you would simply try to transfer to that person the skills you see excellent golfers using. By holding in mind an accomplished performer—a role model—and "seeing" what it is they do that makes them excellent, you can almost always come up with a list of the behaviors you need to encourage and develop in the performer. Likewise, if you have to coach someone to be better at customer service, for example, you need only identify the behaviors that someone with excellent customer service skills employs and then communicate those behaviors with clarity to the person you are trying to improve.

External role models are useful coaching tools too. When IKEA first came to North America, they seeded each store with what they called "culture bearers." These were people who were already engaged in the behaviors company managers wanted to see in all employees. So when new employees wondered how to act, they could turn and watch a culture bearer and learn what a good performance looked like.

During times of workplace upheaval, companies that have a sense of how important role models can be pick out people who adjust quickly to change and train them in what they're looking for so that others have models.

Cage Match: Imagery versus Willpower

Here's another fact concerning imagery: it has beaten willpower in every game ever played!

Willpower is often cited as being central to advancement in high performance, and poor performance is often attributed to a lack of will on the part of the performer. Pioneering psychologist Émile Coué said, "When the imagination and the willpower are in conflict, *it is always the imagination that wins, without exception.*" This is a powerful statement, that imagination is stronger than will. In other words, no matter how badly you want something, if you can't imagine it happening or being able to do it, it isn't going to happen. Coué went on to add, "When the imagination and the willpower are harmoniously pulling in the same direction, irresistible force is the result."

I've been told by more than a few business leaders that their people need to be "hungrier," "want it more," have more drive, more ambition. But most of us won't voluntarily put ourselves in a position where failure will be the certain result. Few people are willing to run full-steam ahead when they cannot see the path. These business leaders would get a better response by reducing their motivational rhetoric and focusing their communication skills on painting clear pictures of what is possible for those under their care. The message "Ya gotta believe" is all well and good, but the person also needs to be able to see that what is being asked of them is at least possible.

It really boils down to this: We can't expect people to self-adjust without a clear picture of what is expected. Decathlon coach Andy Higgins says that expectation is the basis of all successful coaching. There are really two meanings to the word *expectation.* The first is connected to belief: "I

know you can do this!" The second has to do with painting a clear picture
of what is expected, of what constitutes a good performance.

You're a Developer of People—Imagine That!

To be truly effective in any role, the performer needs to have a clear picture
in the mind's eye of what that role looks like, in action, on a daily basis. This
is also true for you! You need to be fully aware of the images generated in
your mind when you think of yourself as a coach, leader or, for that matter,
parent. Without really knowing it you already have some mental representation of these roles. These internal pictures have come from your past experiences with people in these roles, movies you have seen and books you have
read. You also need to be aware of any unconscious bias to which those past
experiences may have contributed, so that you can take that into account in
building a proper picture of what constitutes a good performance in leadership roles.

Some of you will have helpful pictures in your mind because you are fortunate enough to have had splendid role models. But for many of you, a much
more restrictive picture is associated with the word *parent, teacher, leader* or
coach, dramatically limiting your effectiveness with those you are trying to
develop.

Sometimes a restrictive picture can have the opposite effect, however.
Shawn Cornett, who works with Nexen, a large Canadian oil company, wrote
her PhD thesis on effective leaders in learning organizations. One of the things
she discovered was that a good many leaders had developed their skills *because* of spending time under really lousy leaders. They had quietly vowed to
themselves that if they ever had the opportunity to manage, they would never
behave as those leaders did. For example, if they had been micromanaged in
the past, they knew how that felt and didn't micromanage those under their
care. Despite having been brought up in a not-very-pleasant environment,
these leaders took the time to figure out how they wanted to be. So if you
didn't have the good fortune to have had excellent role models, take the
time to form some pictures of how *you* want to be as a leader in your role of
developing others.

Meetings provide a forum for the leader to paint mental pictures
of where employees are going and the actions that will get them there.
Often this is best achieved by asking a series of questions. I worked for

15 years as athletic director at York University's Glendon College in Toronto. In the mid-1980s there were severe cuts to university funding from government sources. One Friday afternoon I was called up to the office of the vice-president of finance and informed that I had to cut 20 percent of my office budget.

On Monday morning I gathered the office and equipment room staffs and told them we would be meeting Friday afternoon in the conference room to discuss ideas on how to reduce our office expenses by 20 percent. I made it clear that I didn't want any ideas at that moment—they were to stockpile them until the Friday meeting. I also let them know that I would be posting questions on the walls related to the 20 percent. The questions were designed to get them thinking about possibilities and to question the status quo—"Is this a task that has to be done?" "Is there another, perhaps cheaper, way of achieving what you are about to copy?"—as well as to increase awareness and clarity about the task before proceeding.

I can honestly say that after Friday's meeting we had greater purchasing power in a budget that had been reduced by 20 percent than we'd had the previous year. It was astounding the number of ideas people came up with to cut costs, save money and generally do things in a more effective manner. I want to emphasize that *none* of these ideas came from me—and there was a good reason for that. I rarely, if ever, used the photocopier, for example, so was not likely to come up with any realistic money-saving ideas in that area. There is always more wisdom in a group than there ever is in any one individual, and the people doing the job usually have the best ideas related to that job.

The most important outcome of the brainstorming was not the 20 percent reduction but the tremendous clarity we all developed about the behaviors we needed to engage in to be cost-effective. When students were being trained for part-time jobs in the office, the equipment room or the swimming pool, I never heard the supervisors, as they were called in those days, say things like "You've got to be cost-effective" or "We really don't want any wastefulness here." What I heard instead were instructions about specific behaviors the students were to engage in that would lead to those outcomes. My role in all this was a facilitative one. As with Robert in his quest to be a better listener, it was as if we had gone into a darkroom with film of what we wanted to achieve and, over the course of the next two hours, gradually developed—together—a picture of what that would look like in action.

Create a Line of Sight

It's important for the individual to be able to see how what they are being asked to do at any given moment is connected either to where they are going and how they are going to get there, or where the entire team is going and how the team is going to reach its end goal. **Commitment levels rise in people who can see a direct connection between what they are doing at this moment and the end goal.**

In working with elite athletes I've noticed that the good coaches always take the time to explain carefully how, for example, a particular weight-room exercise is connected to what they want to achieve and where they ultimately want to go. Athletes who are given a clear line of sight from this bench press in the weight room to that position on the podium are more committed than those who are simply told, "I'm the coach; just do what I say."

A clear line of sight to the end goal is sometimes hampered by the fact that people at lower levels in the workplace hierarchy generally don't have the benefit of all the information upper-level managers are privy to. Let's suppose, to take a simple example, that you and I are working in the same office and our manager encourages us to engage in a new procedure: photocopying on both sides of the page. With you she takes the time to explain that photocopying on both sides of the page, although a small action, will lead to X dollars in savings over the course of a month, and by year's end savings of Y dollars. Your commitment level to photocopying on both sides of the page will be much higher than mine if, upon being given the command, I ask why and am simply told, "Look, Jensen, just do it, okay?"

When we are trying to ignite the Third Factor in a performer, we would do well to remember how important all the whys and wherefores are to us in our own level of commitment. If we are truly trying to develop the other person, it's important to let them see into our thinking about what we are asking them to do, and how that is connected to the bigger picture. This also helps them break things down into the steps necessary in effectively tackling large goals or problems.

The photocopy example above is a simple one, but imagery that connects to the end goal is also an effective way to increase the other person's desire to do something that initially may seem extremely difficult or impossible. Eugene, CEO of a computer chip manufacturing company, asked me to speak at a beginning-of-the-year gathering of all 900 employees of the organization. I arrived early to observe his presentation. He walked on stage dressed in a futuristic outfit and welcomed the audience to the start of the year 2000, although it was actually 1997. He then painted a picture of the year-end figures that had been achieved, making comments like "Back in 1997 we would have thought this was impossible, but people rose to the occasion and were innovative"—and went on to paint a clear and compelling view of the future as if it had already occurred.

After I spoke, the audience split up into work groups and talked about what they might start doing more of, what they should stop doing, and what they needed to learn or acquire in order to reach the vision Eugene had created. In imagery there are no barriers, so people are free to imagine what is possible, get excited and create the means for getting there. The employees painted a believable picture of a staircase that would take them to those 2000 results. (In fact, by the target date they had actually surpassed those results by a good margin and become a major player in the marketplace.)

Encourage the Performer to Translate Words into Images

It is a normal and regular occurrence for athletic coaches to ask athletes what they imagined or felt as they were performing or about to perform. Coaches make continual reference to, and ask questions about, the inner world of the athlete because ultimately that is where excellent performance lies. As we see in the chapter that follows, most of the blocks and clues to the next steps are inside. Olympic coaches understand that what their athletes are imagining is critical. Often it is the very thing that's standing in the way! Why should it be different for any leader working with any performer?

Performers will not improve their competence in any area unless they learn to **translate the instructions** they receive from their coach **into the only language their body comprehends and responds to: Imagery.** When a performer is given feedback, it's important that they take the time to pre-play in their mind, using imagery, the improved action before trying it in the "real" world. A performer rushing into the next attempt saying, "Yeah, yeah, I'll make sure I'm a lot calmer this time" doesn't really improve performance in any way. Remember: the body doesn't speak English, it speaks Imagery. Therefore we need to "tell" the body in a language it can understand: Imagery. In this instance, if performers are to get any better at being calm when it counts, they need to pre-play the performance in their minds.

This is particularly important when dealing with corrections. Anyone who has ever taught anything knows the frustration of correcting one part of a skill or action only to have an error appear in another part. You have the performer focus on projection in public speaking, for example, and an error occurs in their body language or stage presence that wasn't there in the last trial. You move from one correction to another. What causes such slippage? In most cases it's because they have overemphasized the correction in their imagination. The conductor encourages the drums to play louder, but now the strings and horns are drowned out.

To reduce the likelihood of this possibility, good coaches encourage their performers to take a moment after they have received a correction to imagine the correction and then put it back into the whole where it belongs. In the above example the performer would imagine the correction that was given to improve projection, and then imagine a small section of the speech where projection is blended into the other skills that make for good speech-making. Projection is just part of the overall "music" that makes for a good performance.

When you ask a performer what they are imagining, you are really asking to "see" what they are seeing. Gold-medal diver Sylvie Bernier was struggling with a dive prior to her success in the Los Angeles Olympics in 1984. Her coach asked her to write out what she imagined herself doing as she executed the dive. Reading over what she wrote, he saw that at one point in the sequence she had imagined an incorrect arm movement. They made a correction, and the rest is history. This is one of the many reasons why asking questions, as was emphasized in Chapter 2, is so vital. You cannot correct errors you cannot see.

Here are a few tips that will greatly assist you in igniting the Third Factor and helping your performers excel.

Encourage mental rehearsal. It is often hard to find the time and the right situations in which to practice physically some of the more difficult skills that, if worked on and improved, would make the difference to someone's performance, or even their career. Let's say a person you are working with needs to become more assertive and more comfortable in situations involving confronting. Without intentionally going out of your way to irritate a lot of people so they can practice, how can the learner improve? The answer, of course, is to do the repetitions internally. Athletes do this all time.

Set the scene by using some questions around how they would feel and what obstacles they might encounter. Performers will soon be able to generate the emotions they would feel and then play out various ways of being more assertive. Remember, the subconscious mind does not distinguish between a real and an imagined experience—for the body, images are events.

Have performers imagine someone they know who has a high level of competence at the task. My brother Neal is a quieter, more patient parent than I am. I would sometimes ask myself, "How would Neal handle this?" I picked up all kinds of clues about how I might proceed by imagining Neal handling my situation. This particular use of imagery is called *scenario performing.*

Golfer Johnny Miller says that the year he won nine tournaments he had three people playing for him: Lee Trevino, Tony Lima and himself. Each had a very different swing. Miller would hit the ball very straight, whereas Lima's shots tended to fade and Trevino's to draw. Miller points out that for every situation on the golf course, one of those three people had the right swing, adding (tongue-in-cheek, I'm sure) that there was no way all three guys were going to be playing poorly on the same day!

Ask performers about their end goal, their dreams and their vision. Ask what they see as being possible. Decathlon coach Andy Higgins says it sometimes takes him years to convince talented young athletes that they can compete at the world-class level. He told me an amazing story about David Steen, who won the bronze medal in the Seoul Olympic Games in 1988. (We now know that David was, in fact, the gold medalist, as those ahead of him were using steroids.) Here's Andy's story:

"The best coaches paint pictures, word pictures, live pictures, but the biggest one is inviting their athletes to imagine, to dream. In David Steen's case I got him to 'see' what was possible for himself. The first step was to get him out of Cal Berkeley and into a situation of thinking about his long-term interests and how he could be an Olympian. At the time his focus was on winning the NCAA. The biggest thing I was able to do was to help him see himself standing on the podium, clean (drug-free).

"It was one of the most profound experiences I've ever had. When he came to us he was more talented than even I realized. I went home and did the scoring tables. Holy smoke! When I added up realistic scores for him, four or five years down the road, the total came to 8707. [British Olympic gold medalist] Daly Thompson's world record at the time was 8716.

"I consulted Zoltan, another decathlon coach, and he agreed with each individual event assessment, but he couldn't believe the total was over 8700. 'Not possible,' he said. 'Give me those forms.' I watched him pull out his scoring table and calculator and add them all up. After uttering an emphatic Hungarian expletive, he said, 'It *is* 8700!'

"And just at that moment, like in a B movie, Steen walked in the door. 'David, sit down,' I said. 'We were just talking about you.' We walked him through our projections for each event, and he mostly agreed, although when we got to the shot-put David argued for his limitations. Zoltan said, 'David, every Grade 9 schoolgirl has better technique than you, but this number will be possible after four years of working with a world-class throwing coach.'

"'Yeah,' he says, 'okay, you're right.' We go through them all, and, with no other discussion, he agrees to all the individual event projections.

"'David,' I say, 'what do you think they add up to?' Now it's like Zoltan without the accent.

"'It's got to be 8200 or 8300.'

"And I'm smiling at this point and I say, 'No, David, it's 87 . . .' I do not get the next two digits out.

"He says, 'I could never do that.' He knew enough to know that 8700 was just a bit short of Daly's record, but he couldn't see himself achieving it despite the fact he had just agreed to every single component that added up to 8700!

"That is the biggest thing we face with every human being we deal with. Somewhere in there are these crazy limiting beliefs in spite of the fact that they 'know' better. So it's an issue of constantly changing the ability to see oneself being able to do whatever it is."

Salespeople, in particular, relate to this story because they are often overwhelmed by the end goal—the year-end target—even though they can imagine, to some degree, achieving the month-end numbers that add up to the year-end totals. But regardless of which department your people are in, they likely all share the common fear of the big targets, which is why breaking things down is so important. Good coaches remember to give a picture of performance goals rather than just the end goal.

Imagery Exercises

I want to give you an imagery experience here, but the problem is that reading the page at the same time won't be practical or convenient if you prefer to do the exercises with your eyes closed. So we'll compromise. I'll give you a small imagery appetizer here if you agree to go to www.ignitingthethirdfactor.com for the main course. There you'll be talked through the exercises for an easier and more satisfying experience.

Read the lines below starting with 1. Close your eyes after each one, then, taking your time, let yourself experience the idea. Try to suspend the judge in you that wonders whether you're doing it right. You are. Just do it.

1. Smell: You're filling up your automobile with gasoline; imagine pulling the trigger on the nozzle. The strong smell of gasoline rises to your nose.
2. Touch: You're sitting beside a cat or a dog and stroking its fur. Notice what it feels like.
3. Taste: Try to experience in your imagination the taste, temperature and texture of a banana . . . then celery . . . and finally, yogurt.
4. Sight: Imagine each of the following: a gold triangle . . . a blue five-pointed star . . . a pen slowly writing your name on paper.
5. Hearing: Hear a squeaking door . . . rain falling . . . someone calling your name.

Potential Obstacles and How to Overcome Them

Using imagery to enhance performance sounds great in theory, and it does work. But reality has a way of testing us when we're trying something new. Our clients are always happy to point out why something will be difficult to implement (see obstacle 1 below), so I thought I'd bring up these perceived obstacles now in case you thought I hadn't taken them into account.

1. **Lack of belief in themselves.** The toughest obstacle is the one Andy spoke about—the belief that someone can actually achieve what you're asking them to do. This is common even in the workplace. When someone isn't performing or expresses hesitation about be-

ing able to perform, we often think it's a question of competence. It may be that, but it could also be a lack of confidence.

Confidence is affected by many things. Some performers may not have been confident when you hired them. Or maybe they were, but over time, as duties have gradually changed from what they were hired to do, or new responsibilities have been added, or there's a faster pace or more pressure, or a change in team members, confidence can suffer. You don't want to assume confidence any more than you want to assume competence. And it takes both of those to be successful. One of your roles as a leader is to build confidence in your performers. Being sensitive to people's self-esteem needs is just plain good business.

It is also true that what you, as a coach, imagine has a profound impact on your confidence and therefore on your performance as a leader. We tend to do what we imagine. If you want to be confident as a coach, you have to think about and imagine what that looks like and be able to translate it for the body and feelings. You can't do what you can't imagine, so it's a good idea, particularly in key situations or environments where you have to perform well, to be conscious of your own imagery. Because your body language is so important in communicating your confidence in others, you need to exude confidence yourself.

2. **Lack of time.** Many managers believe they don't have time to create pictures for effective communication because the business world moves so quickly. But imagery, when used effectively, is actually a communication shortcut. When you have to keep repeating a message because you weren't effective the first time, you're not saving any time at all!

Employees in most organizations develop an imagery vocabulary that summarizes certain behaviors. I heard a comical example of this while on a corporate retreat with a company in the financial field. It was about 10:30 at night and I was with a group of the managers enjoying a cold beverage or two in the bar. One of the longer-term managers said, "Let's have one more and get out of here. We don't want to 'pull a Fred.'"

Several of us inquired what the "pull a Fred" comment was all about. What followed was a long, funny story about a former manager named Fred, whose misbehavior at this annual retreat a few years earlier—involving too much alcohol, a colleague and the hot tub—was interrupted by a senior VP. "Pulling a Fred" became an imagery-based warning that kept managers who were interested in future advancement from indulging in activities that would lead to embarrassment and possible unemployment.

3. **Unreasonable goals.** If the picture you create is unattainable, your performers will still come up short, so it's important to use imagery in the context of reasonable, attainable performance. If you don't, obstacle 1 (lack of belief) will come into play, negatively affecting the outcome.

4. **Your perspective/their perspective.** Obstacle 4, perspective, is made up, in part, of obstacles 1 and 3. It's important to understand the performers' perspectives, because that will tell you what images they're running and what you have to deal with. How are they seeing things, and do you need to adjust the imagery you're using to communicate with them? Asking questions and getting them to create clear pictures of what success would look like or what constitutes a good performance will help you "see" what *they* are imagining.

Back to our meeting. As with achieving excellence in any domain, an effective meeting starts in the imagination of the leader. Do you have a clear picture of how you want your team to interact, your meetings to run? If, once the meeting is over, people are raving—yes, raving—about it, ask yourself what happened in there that made it so good. What this information on imagery should be telling you is that concepts like "I want to involve my people more in decision making" need to be broken down into what you, the leader, would see them doing and hear them saying if that were a reality. Then—and this is critical because that behavior will not come out of the sky—you need to see what you did and what you said that made it so successful. What actions did you take that led to their behavior and the successful meeting?

Extinguishers lack imagination, therefore:
- Their people are frustrated because they lack clarity on what to do and how to do it.
- They demotivate, put stress on people by harping on the end goal and fail to connect the achievement of performance goals to the end goal.
- They *demand* and *tell* with no knowledge of what people need to do to internalize and act on those commands.

To be an Igniter remember this!
- Paint clear pictures of what is desired.
- Create a line of sight from individual actions to shared or end goals.
- Encourage the performer to translate words into images.

Author: Well, what are your thoughts on imagery now?

Editor: I'm just beginning to see the possibilities. It certainly was much more practical than I imagined, and I keep thinking there must be some trick or faulty assumption that I'm missing.

Author: I remember when I first really got it, when I first really grasped the significance of the whole area of imagery and its role not only in developing others but also, and perhaps even more so, in my own development. I kept thinking "How could I have missed this?" It's so simple to understand and yet it has many layers to it and is definitely multidimensional. It was as if I had uncovered a secret. But when I listened to coaches talking and performers being interviewed, I started to notice continual references to imagery, vision and so on.

Editor: I'm not there yet, but I can certainly see where you're coming from. It just seems too easy, too obvious, and I can't believe I've missed it either. Maybe it's because I'm so much younger than you are!

Author: I'm not sure how significant this is, but most of the really good in-depth literature on imagery comes from the pre-television era. Concert cellist Yo Yo Ma refers to imagery as the forgotten language of our youth. With the advent of video games, high-definition television and the like, there is concern in some quarters that we are not engaging the minds of our children in the imaginary world. Just a few years ago children had the fun of providing the movement and sounds of a toy automobile, whereas today the toy does all that for them. Anyway, you haven't missed it because it's clear you're beginning to "see" the possibilities even as we speak. The key, in my opinion, is not to let that slip away. It was Winston Churchill who said man stumbles over the truth every so often, picks himself up, brushes himself off and continues on his way. We will make frequent references back to imagery in what follows.

6

Uncover and Work Through Blocks

Author: Do you ever hit a roadblock on something and just feel stymied, unable to make any progress?

Editor: You mean like me trying to get you moving on these last few chapters? Okay, okay, just kidding. Of course I've been blocked. Who hasn't?

Author: What do you do when you feel you're stuck and not making any progress?

Editor: I have a few close friends I talk to when I'm stuck or can't seem to get going on something. There's nothing really fancy about it. I talk; they listen and ask questions. Eventually things seem to get clear after a bit and I figure out what to do. Why?

Author: I'll respond to "why" in a moment. This is interesting. What do they do that helps you eventually get clarity?

Editor: As I said, they listen and ask questions and I talk, and talk, and talk. Now that you have me thinking about it, they do stop every so often to see if they've understood what I'm telling them. I get the feeling you're about to ask me how they do that, so I'll answer that now. They simply put into their own words what they think I've said and check it out with me.

Author: Good friends to have! Tell me, have you tried this with anyone else, and if so, how well did it work?

Editor: I tried it once, and only once, with my husband, and that was a dismal failure. We ended up in a huge argument, which was unfortunate because his intentions were good. He really did want to help me, but he moved into problem-solving mode almost immediately, and all I wanted to do was talk about the issue so we could both understand it before we moved to a solution. I think one of the problems was that, as you know, he works in the same field as I do. My friends know very little about my work world, so sometimes they ask what at first appear to be very naïve questions. But the funny thing is, they—both the questions and the friends—really do help.

Author: I think, from what you've said, that you could write a good deal of this chapter. In my workshops I often ask participants, "When was the last time someone gave you 45 minutes of undivided attention to help you solve an issue that was critical to you?" The silence that follows says more than words ever could.

Editor: Thanks for the vote of confidence, but I am not writing the chapter. Nice try.

UNCOVER AND WORK THROUGH BLOCKS

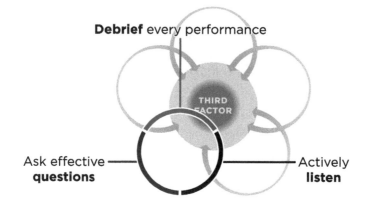

One of the many wise sayings attributed to the Chinese philosopher Lao-Tse is the pronouncement "What's in the way is the way." This simple statement has given me tremendous awareness and has become a practical diagnostic tool for me. In working with hundreds of athletes and coaches and delivering thousands of speeches and seminars over the past 25 years, I have either quoted Lao-Tse's wisdom or used it as a diagnostic tool. If a figure skater, for example, lands six triple jumps in a morning practice but only one in the evening competition because she gets nervous or anxious, what do we work on? Do we work on jumping technique? It's clear from the morning practice that she can do the jumps. So we work on what's in the way: she gets nervous or anxious in competition.

Let's pause for a little spot quiz here. Do we work on not being nervous, not being anxious? Not if we were paying attention during the imagery chapter! Remember the "don't buy cheese," "don't buy corn" shopping list of items *not* to buy? The same principle applies in this situation. If imagery is the language of performance, then rather than focus on the negatives—the "nots" and the "don'ts"—we go for what we *do* want. We work on the positive goals of being strong, calm and confident.

Many years ago I was speaking at a conference for children with learning difficulties and I heard a wonderfully engaging speaker named Sol Gordon. At one point, referring to mentally challenged teenagers, he said, "Don't block a block with a block." His point was that when you are frustrated that something isn't going well because the other person is blocked, blurting out the equivalent of "Look, I don't care, just do it" only makes your task of developing this person more difficult. By adding a second block—your impatience—you have succeeded only in compounding the problem. Good coaches don't block a block with another block. They find out what's in the way and focus on that.

Conflict and Disintegration

Conflict is an essential component of Dabrowski's theory and the Third Factor. When someone is blocked, there is a tremendous opportunity to engage the Third Factor and help developmentally. This is when learning can really accelerate. But for a new, higher level of integration to occur, there first has to be disintegration. To use an image, the old "building" must be taken down before the new one can be built. This developmental process begins with conflict, which is usually external, although as the progression continues the conflict becomes more internal. It may start out as "I can't get this right," but once you engage with the person you may discover it has moved inside to "I'm not sure I can do this." As we see in the examples that follow, that's when inner work can lead to moving to a new level.

I asked decathlon coach Andy Higgins what actions he takes when one of his athletes is not improving but is blocked or regressing.

"I call one of my sport psych friends!" he joked. "But seriously, it becomes more of a counseling intervention on my part. Engaging with the person is central to all coaching. A whole lot of what passes as coaching—and in many situations it's pretty effective up to quite a high level—is the ability to create and manage supportive environments, teach skills, create learning environments, inspire and motivate. All powerful stuff. But when these coaches finally come up against a block—whatever is getting in the way of the next step—all kinds of them can't go there or are afraid to go there or weren't trained to go there or never thought of it themselves, or have this belief that that's just the way it is. How many athletes 'ceiling out' as a result of that kind of failing on the coach's part?

"So how do you deal with it? By the end of my career I knew this: you have to begin on day one. If you do it right from day one, you don't run into a big block four or five years down the road. It's about self-awareness: recognizing old beliefs and attitudes that are no longer useful and are getting in the way, then building on that awareness, using techniques such as relaxation, visualization and imagery so that you're looking at the issue from all sides. If you build that into the program from the very beginning, problems [blocks] down the road will be minimal."

There are times when it's obvious to both the performer and the coach that there is something in the way, that progress toward a goal has stopped and that the person's Third Factor has been temporarily extinguished. At other times it may be painfully obvious to the manager but not to the performer. It may indeed even get to the point where it is necessary for the manager to confront the performer about it. But there are also times when it isn't obvious to either party that there is a block. Sometimes an assumption is made that disguises or hides the block. Let me give you an example.

Prior to one of the Olympic Games, I was working with a young female swimmer who was hoping to qualify for the national team. Just a year earlier this had looked like a foregone conclusion to everyone: herself, her parents and her coach. Her history was one of continual improvement. Each year her times had improved substantially. But in the six-month period from June to December of the year before the Olympics, she had gone through puberty, and her body was now significantly changed. Gone was the streamlined pre-puberty "swimming torpedo," replaced by a more curvaceous model on a more substantial frame.

The young woman's swim times stagnated or in some cases regressed slightly. At the same time, her social life improved and she was spending more time hanging out with her peers. Various reports from the "front" indicated that her parents thought she had become lazy and her coach thought she wasn't pushing herself. She herself was totally frustrated with the lack of progress. I met with her several times, and it became clear to me that although she logically understood what was happening to her physically, she was also attributing her lack of progress to other possibilities. Specifically, she wondered whether she was talented enough or had what it took to be an Olympian.

Many athletes—perhaps most—don't really want to know the answer to that question. Rather than truly find out whether or not they are sufficiently talented, they opt for less effort and a future explanation that implies they *could* have made it but didn't want to push themselves that hard.

This, of course, is true not just of athletes but also of anyone who has initial success in something and then runs up against a time when progress ceases to be easy. One of my children had a similar experience in connection with learning a second language, and another with mathematics.

I wasn't making any real progress with the swimmer. Conversation was difficult because there was really nothing specific we could talk about. So I asked Sandra, my wife, to see her. Here is Sandra's description of how she was able to counsel this young woman to help her overcome a block, reignite her Third Factor and make the Olympic team.

"I asked her, 'So the coach thinks you're lazy and your parents think you're not motivated. Are those things true?' She said they weren't true, so I asked, 'What makes your coach *think* you're lazy?' and she talked about how she wasn't swimming the same times and progress had halted.

"Through a series of questions we got to the fact that she wasn't working as hard any more and that was probably why the coach thought she was lazy and her parents thought she wasn't motivated. When I asked her why she wasn't working as hard, she said, 'Because I don't think I have what it takes to go all the way.' I then asked her what that felt like, to be swimming when she didn't feel she had what it takes to succeed at the highest level.

"After she described how she felt, I asked her, 'Where in the body do you feel that?' I encouraged her to let an image come that captured that feeling for her. She came up with an image of a wall, and I asked her if there was any way around, over or through the wall. She said there was no way around it and no way through it. I asked her if she could climb over it. She said she didn't know.

"I said, 'Why don't you try? Why don't you just climb the wall and see what happens?' In her imagery she was climbing the wall, and I asked her what it was like. She said, 'It's really hard. I'm having a hard time and I keep slipping back.' I encouraged her to stay with it and see what happened. She continued to climb the wall, and it was very hard, but eventually she got to the top. She laughed a bit and I asked her what had happened.

"She said, 'I just fell off the wall.' 'On what side?' I asked. 'On the other side' was her joyous reply. 'What's happening now?' I wanted to know. 'I'm running,' she said. 'How does that feel?' I asked her. Her response: 'It feels great!'

"When we came out of the imagery, we understood that the process for improving had become really hard and that what she'd been thinking was 'If it's that hard, I mustn't be any good.' That's when she told me that swimming had always been so easy for her, but when it got hard she thought it meant she 'wasn't good enough.'

"At this point the nature of our conversation changed, because now she had a different question to answer. The question wasn't 'Am I talented enough?' but 'Am I prepared to do the work it's going to take to climb that wall, knowing it's going to be hard and that I'm going to slip back occasionally but that eventually I'll make progress again?'"

This swimmer's situation demonstrates something that is not always obvious: when talented performers hit a certain point in their development and it gets difficult for them, one of the interpretations they put on it is that they are not talented enough. That was a huge revelation for me.

The Need for Patience

There is a lot to learn, and one of the key steps in the learning process is **accepting the blocks for what they are: normal lessons on the developmental path.** Toronto Raptor coach Sam Mitchell, who was coach of the year in 2007, was discussing with the media the struggles of the player Andrea Bargnani in his second year in the league. "What's wrong with him struggling?" he said. "What's wrong with that? Haven't we all gone through some struggles? And what does it do? It instills character.

"Why don't we have patience? I don't expect y'all [in the media] to. But we who are in charge are supposed to have the patience to understand that that's the process some young players require. The struggle makes you dig deeper. You learn something about yourself. And then when you come out of it, you're kind of proud of yourself. That's a good thing for a young player."

What Sam was also pointing out—and it's a valid point to make here before we head into the three practical steps for identifying and overcoming blocks—is that we often judge competence too early. In our desire for our performers to deliver, we make assessments on competence that in the end not only don't trigger the Third Factor in the performer but actually inhibit it.

Let me put this into a work context. Steve Earle is our sales manager, responsible for generating our revenue and for creating and maintaining our relationships with clients. Several months after we hired Steve I was teaching a program at Queen's University with Peggy Baumgartner, who heads up our training division. Steve had come to us from IBM, where he had spent 21 years, a good many of them in charge of the sales and marketing school.

Peggy and I were kvetching about how long it was taking Steve to "get with it" and get the sales rolling. "How much time does he have to invest and how many programs does he have to see before he can sell them?" was our general lament. Fortunately, we reminded each other of one of the key tenets we teach in our coaching program, under a section called "The Transition Curve." The point is that when people are going through a change, as Steve certainly was after 21 years at IBM, it's too easy for leaders, in their need to get things done, to be relieved of some of the workload, or, in this instance, see sales results that reflect the investment they have made, to judge competence too early and slow down or halt the progress that *is* being made. By judging too early, you risk creating a self-fulfilling prophecy. Fortunately, we were able to see that we should practice what we preached, and within a year we were dealing with the challenge of bringing new presenters on board to do all the work that Steve's sales had generated!

There are certain key things good coaches do to ignite the Third Factor and thereby help their performers continue to develop while dealing with blocks: they debrief every performance; they learn to ask discerning questions to uncover the block; and they listen actively to the responses.

Debrief Every Performance

Every once in a while someone, hopefully only metaphorically, hits you between the eyes with a two-by-four of an observation you can't believe has escaped you until this late in your life. I had such a moment in my interview with decathlon coach Andy Higgins, who told me, **"If we do not debrief and evaluate every performance, we are in no position to evaluate and learn from the disasters."**

He was discussing a heptathlete (women do heptathlons, 7 events; men decathlons, 10 events) he was working with years ago. After a particularly poor performance he asked her questions related to confidence and her inner world. "How were you feeling before that event?" "What sorts of things were you thinking about prior to the long jump?" "Did you have any doubts or negative thoughts that might have affected your performance?" On the surface, with no sense of history or context, these appear to be appropriate questions designed to help the athlete perform better next time. That is not how they were received. In the period immediately following her disappointing performance she became increasingly agitated and frustrated with Andy's questions, finally blurting out, "What are you saying? That I'm a choke?"

After hearing Andy's story, I changed my approach. In my work with Olympic athletes I now set up meetings to take place prior to important practices, after important practices, prior to competitive events and after competitive events. These are not long meetings; they're 5- to 10-minute get-togethers for touching base and giving athletes the opportunity to talk about how they are feeling, their level of competence and other questions relevant to their particular situation. Setting up these meetings ahead of time ensures that the athletes accept them as normal, routine occurrences, and avoids leaving them with the impression that we've suddenly called a meeting because we think they're choking.

In a variation of this practice, Canadian Olympic women's hockey coach Mel Davidson sets up such meetings to include not only the players but also the dozen or so staff people (doctor, physical therapist, massage therapist, media director, sport psychologist). But while we are all welcome at those game-day team meetings and film sessions, she makes it clear that either we attend all of them, or none of them. She doesn't want a sudden crowd appearing prior to the gold-medal game and by their very presence giving the players the message that this is suddenly critical.

I asked Andy about the general principle of uncovering blocks and its level of importance. His reply: "The first thing anyone who is to be coached has to agree on is that they will engage in this process of self-awareness and reflection, introspection and evaluation because they need to be fully aware of how they are responding to what is going on in every situation. If they are successful, they need to be aware of what was going on (What was I thinking? How did I feel? How did I act?). It's easy and pleasant to do when we're successful, but often we *don't* do it and therefore don't reinforce it."

Debriefing Is an Investment

If you don't take the time to debrief performances one-on-one with your people, then how will they know specifically how they are doing and what needs to happen? How will they know what they need to continue doing, what they need to stop doing, start doing, let go of, or change? It takes time, you say? Yes, it does, but it's an investment of that valuable and finite commodity that will yield an important dividend: time, and lots of it over time!

I'm not going to pretend that this kind of debriefing is easy to do in the work world. Athletic coaches at the highest level see it as part of their job, but very few managers have the time or opportunity to attend to it in the same "hands-on" way. Often, other responsibilities take precedence. Another reason debriefing is easier in sport is that the coach usually witnesses the performance. But even though it's harder to debrief a performance in the business environment, the need for it is no less valid. The more performances you debrief, the more adept you will become at assessing and providing effective feedback on the poor or disappointing ones. More important, it will lead to greater openness to change on the part of the performer. Debriefing performances and giving competent, relevant feedback is what coaching (and good managing) is all about. Igniting occurs best through engagement—through being there as much as possible.

Getting into the habit of touching base with your performers to find out what they are doing and how it is going makes good business sense. Studies on the office environment reveal that the better managers have more interactions with their people. When those interactions focus on development through performance-related coaching sessions, research also tells us that successful behaviors tend to "stick" and produce much better results. A study by Public Personnel Management found that training increased productivity by 22 percent, but when that training was combined with coaching, the increase was an astounding 88 percent.

Coaching as Problem Solving

Bob Nardelli, CEO of The Home Depot, hit the nail on the head when he said, "I absolutely believe that unless people are coached, they never reach their maximum potential." In a comment more specific to this chapter on blocks, John Russell, managing director for Harley-Davidson's European division, said, "I never cease to be amazed at the power of the coaching process to draw out the skills or talent previously hidden within an individual, and how it invariably finds a way to solve a problem previously thought unsolvable."

Block-free Meetings

Let's go back to the meeting as a model for examining how these concepts work in real life. What blocks us from having good meetings? Why are so many meetings so inefficient and such a waste of one of our most valuable resources: time? The answer is profound in its simplicity: we rarely work on them. Very few leaders focus on getting better at conducting meetings and on helping those in attendance learn to work more effectively in groups. Think about this for a minute. We spend an inordinate amount of time in groups, complain about how many meetings we have to attend, wish we had more time for other things—and never really focus in any constructive way on becoming skilled at conducting meetings so that we get more done in less time and move on to other challenges.

I need to tell you a story here. Yes, *need*—it's in me and wants to get out! The summer before I was a senior in high school and for four summers while at university I worked underground in a mine. The first year I worked with a man named Emile. Every day at lunchtime I would take out the lunch my mother had made for me and listen to Emile complain bitterly about his peanut butter and jam sandwich. You have to imagine him doing this in a wonderful French accent. "Bloody peanut butter and g&^%## jam sandwich again. Every day the same &^%$# sandwich, I don't believe it." This would go on, in brilliant Technicolor, for two or three minutes each day.

Finally one day I said to him, "Emile, why don't you have your wife make you something else?"

"Oh," he responded, "I'm not married, Peter. I make my own lunch."

That's how I feel when I hear people griping about, as John Cleese put it, "meetings, bloody meetings." We all make our own meeting/team experience, our own version of peanut butter and jam. So let's talk about dealing with the blocks to good meetings. Andy Higgins's advice above is to debrief every performance. A meeting is a performance, so it needs to be debriefed. But before I tell you how to do that, I'd like to discuss teams.

Perhaps the biggest myth ever perpetrated on any work group is the expression "There is no 'I' in team." The truth is, the experience of being on any team is wrought with "I" and "we" issues. It is part of what makes group work so challenging and why there are so few high-performing teams. Balancing I/we, competition/cooperation, give/take is what the team experience is all about. Most people are not naturally good at this, which is why meetings go off schedule, old issues are revisited, the atmosphere grows more and more uncomfortable, and so on.

As a leader you can make a real contribution to better teams and meetings by focusing on two things: helping individuals get better at managing themselves ("I"), and helping each member learn how to work more effectively with others ("we").

You debrief by asking questions that focus on both the "I" and the "we" of the team/group. Asking each person simple questions at the end of every meeting builds the awareness that allows the team to get better. Here are the four suggested questions, the first two focusing on the "I," the second two on the "we."

"What do you need more of?"
- "What do you need less of?"
- "What are we doing well?"
- "What needs work?"

You only get better at things you consciously work on. When a participant says they need more cooperation and less conflict, you learn something about the impact of the meeting on an individual. And their answer to the "we" questions can be just as revealing: "What went well was the discussion on the new project. It was clear everyone had done the pre-meeting reading and the solution came very quickly as a result. What needs work is our timing. We run out of time and short-change some important issues at the end of the meeting. Perhaps we could move those up to next week's agenda, where they'll get the time they deserve." From that you learn something about group effectiveness and how you can all work together to improve.

Some amazing things happen when a leader facilitates the answering of these questions in the last 10 minutes of every meeting. Almost immediately, things progress more smoothly because there is a forum at the end in which people know they can be heard, so they hold their concerns rather than disrupt the flow of the meeting and take up valuable time. The compulsion to react declines as well because there is a clear understanding that even comments that might be difficult to hear, such as "I need less criticism from some team members," focus on the future, the next meeting, decreasing the likelihood of people getting mired in the past.

You will likely feel a great temptation to haul out the "no time" excuse here; we all do. But if it makes meetings more effective, increases the commitment of those present, and cuts down dramatically on time-wasting dysfunctional behavior, can you really afford *not* to debrief meetings? It is, indeed, time well spent.

Ask Effective Questions

In the chapter on communication, I talk about the importance of asking questions and being able to listen actively. In the section on trust I point out that the ability to ask probing questions and to listen attentively are vital in developing a relationship of trust with another person. In the section that follows we look at the skill of active listening as it relates to dealing with adversity. Here we delve into developing the ability to ask the sorts of questions that can lead to uncovering a block.

As previously mentioned, I have been strongly influenced by the work of a colleague of mine, Sir John Whitmore, in London, England, and his excellent book *Coaching for Performance*. John developed a one-on-one coaching tool called the GROW exercise, which we at Performance

Coaching use in all our coaching workshops. GROW is an acronym for **G**oal, **R**eality, **O**ptions and **W**ill. Over the past 25 years, John and his colleagues have refined a series of questions in each of these four areas. When asked by a coach using the skill of active listening, these questions lead performers to come up with fitting solutions to their own problems.

Questions to GROW On

If the GROW exercise interests you, you can find a full version of it in John Whitmore's book *Coaching for Performance*. The exercise really grows out of four basic questions:

- What is your goal? What do you want to accomplish?
- What is happening now (including "What have you done about this so far and what results did that produce?")?
- What options do you have? (Here you are trying to elicit a list of all possibilities, and you conclude by asking if the person would like a suggestion from you.)
- What are you going to do, and when are you going to do it?

After one of our workshops, I received an e-mail from one of the participants, Kent Brown, the chief financial officer for a large Canadian company, concerning the use of the GROW exercise with one of his employees. Here are some of his comments:

"I thought you would be interested in some direct feedback on the GROW process/tool. I used it this morning with a staff member and had my HR manager attend the meeting. It is an incredibly effective tool and lifts an enormous weight off my shoulders in problem-solving/coaching. It is so rewarding when someone walks out of a meeting with a way forward that she has come up with herself and is truly committed to. It's awesome!"

The HR manager who witnessed the one-on-one coaching session e-mailed her comments and congratulations to Kent: ". . . It meant a lot to that employee to be heard and understood. I definitely got a lot out of your strategy—listening, asking the right questions, coaching her through the problem to come up with her own solutions. You were great!"

The following is a short case study concerning one participant's experience with the GROW exercise in a workshop.

John, a senior manager in the municipal office of a large Canadian city, who attended one of our coaching workshops, knows first-hand the power of uncovering the *real* block. The week before he was scheduled to attend our workshop, John's boss was let go unexpectedly. The departure of this man, who was well-liked by many people, including John, sent shock waves through the office and left John reeling. Despite having had no input into the decision, he was worried that the people who reported to him would see it as a power play on his part to move into his boss's role.

At the workshop, John was partnered in the GROW exercise with Jane, a senior manager at a technology company in Ohio. He explained that he had some extremely important issues to discuss with his employees upon his return and needed a plan for how best to approach the discussion. Over the course of the GROW session, however, a different issue emerged. Through the use of questions such as "What if you found out that your employees were happy about you having this opportunity?" John discovered that the real block was his own ambivalence. "I realized that it was really me who was feeling that the process hadn't been fair," he said, "and I was questioning whether I wanted to be involved in the organization any more."

With the real block out on the table, John was able to brainstorm potential solutions that would attack the root problem and narrow in on an action plan. A month later, John reported that he had stepped up into his boss's role with a clear head and the support of his employees. "Once the problem was reframed in a different way, it was easy for me to see where the solutions lay," he said.

Stay in Touch

From time to time we interview workshop participants and create case studies that we publish in our newsletter *IGNITE!*, which is e-mailed to our clients every three months. The newsletter also contains articles on topics our clients indicate are important to them, an ask-the-expert column and a podcast by me. You can sign up for *IGNITE!* by going to my website at www.peterjensen.ca.

Often the performer who is stagnated or stuck lacks clarity on the real problem. We're really back to an imagery issue again in that it is impossible to see your way out of something you do not clearly understand. Once people uncover what is blocking them, it is so much easier to imagine a course of action to get over or around what is in the way. When people have been struggling with something for a period of time, they often attribute their failure to act to a lack of willpower, desire or confidence. Others, particularly their managers and leaders, often make similar assumptions—sometimes even questioning the employee's level of competence.

As we discovered in the imagery section, imagination beats willpower every single time. No amount of willpower will overcome a block until we are able to see clearly what is in the way and imagine the solution. This is an important point and it's easy to overlook. All too often the block is in the imagination. I am a coach and I know how long it took *me* to grasp this concept.

Let's talk a bit about the role of active listening in helping someone uncover and work through a block.

Listen Actively

In Chapter 2 we covered the key skills in active listening. When someone is struggling with a challenge, many coaches tend to want to move quickly into problem-solving mode. Any one of us with even a small dose of ego loves to be Sherlock Holmes and save the day in a display of problem-solving brilliance. (Indeed, moving back to imagery for a moment, many of us have a mental picture of leader and coach as knowledgeable problem-solver and answer-provider. One of the purposes of this book is to assist you in forming a different mental picture of what exceptional coaches do.) But when you reflect back to the other person what you understand them to be saying, you're creating a powerful problem-solving environment. You're helping that person develop clarity around the true nature of the issue with which they're dealing, and because you are also gaining that clarity yourself, once they have exhausted their own ideas, you are in a position to help them with your own input. You can really hit the nail on the head because your listening has helped you "see" the entire breadth and scope of the issue and all its complexities. Listening provides you with clues to unravel the mystery, and puts you in a position to be an exceptional coach.

I know, I know—you've heard this before. Repetition is a great reinforcer of the message, though, especially when presented with slight variations. I also want to remind you that your very presence—choosing to be present to another human being, especially one who is experiencing a difficulty or a block—is powerful in and of itself. Often when we're stuck, what we really want is to talk to someone about it. We don't want them to move instantly into problem-solving mode. We first just want them to understand, truly understand, all that we're going through. This really helps trigger the Third Factor.

It has been my observation that people don't instantly blurt out what's wrong. To find out what the real issue is, you need to **create a safe, reflective environment** in which to get your performers talking—and keep them talking. They need to know that you know where they are "at" and what they are going through. This is why the *active* part of listening is so important. You are not only paying attention and trying to understand them, but you're also letting them know you're "getting it" by feeding back your understanding of what they are saying. This encourages deeper dialogue. People dig much deeper and get to the real issue when they are comfortable and when trust is present.

Of course there's another reason why active listening is important. You need to know what's in the way in order to ignite the Third Factor!

Extinguishers are blocked when it comes to blocks!
- They only debrief when things go wrong, well after the fact or ineffectively, leaving their people floundering.
- They tend to tell, giving their interpretation of what is going on and rarely seeking information from the performer.
- They seem to have been born devoid of ears—at least ears that work!

To be an Igniter remember this!
- Debrief every performance.
- Ask effective questions.
- Listen actively.

Editor: That chapter really explained a lot, and I'm beginning to see how imagery is involved here as well. Many times the block could simply be a lack of imagination, or at least an inability on the part of the performer to "see." I also appreciate my friends more, their great questions and, as you put it, their presence. With time being so precious in today's work world it's a gift to be given undivided attention.

Author: Time is a commodity we don't seem to have enough of, but here's the interesting thing. If the leader takes the time to uncover the block and the performer goes away with a commitment to do something about it, then that is time well spent. If we don't take the time to find out what the real issue is, none of our solutions will work, and in fact we'll be robbed of time in other ways: 10 minutes in a meeting, 5 minutes sending an e-mail, 8 minutes in a hallway conversation. And that's just the time spent by you, the leader. How much time is lost by the performer in uncertainty, preoccupation and trying to figure things out?

Editor: Well, we can't invent more time, can we.

Author: No, we can't—but we can use the time we do have much more effectively. Every conversation we have with someone in our organization is a chance to clarify something or help them get clarity, increase their competence through effective feedback, or give them some ownership or recognition, which in turn ignites their desire to get better, do more. Perhaps our most important role as leaders is to remove the blocks—the organizational ones as well as those in the performer—so that others can perform at higher levels with greater ease.

Editor: I feel a stump speech coming on. Let's move to the next chapter.

7

Embrace Adversity

Editor: Are we talking about embrace as in hugging, or a more WWE version, as in squeeze into submission and eliminate?

Author: It's more of a "get your arms around it" idea—accept it, pick yourself up, get an accurate description of reality, and then act in ways that make the most of what you have and what the situation offers.

Editor: Nietzsche's "what doesn't kill me makes me stronger"?

Author: Ahh . . . we may be on the same page. I forgot you majored in philosophy!

Editor: All kidding aside, it took me a long time to "embrace" that notion.

Author: How so?

Editor: Where do I start? In the past, in any situation that wasn't going well or where things didn't work out the way I wanted them to—in other words, I was facing adversity—my first reaction was to blame others or work harder—do more of what I was doing and try to do it better. I had a philosophy professor sit me down one day and say, "Sue, if you took half the energy you put into telling me how unfair it all is and tried to work harder at unraveling and acting on the lesson this disappointment presents you with, not only would you be stronger, but it would also make it a lot easier for the rest of us to help you and work with you.

Author: Did that help?

Editor: No, not initially; it just irritated me. One day I was reading about Jerry Garcia, late of The Grateful Dead . . ..

Author: Are you a Deadhead?

Editor: Yeah, I really like their music—but we can talk music another time. I read this interview where Jerry was talking about change and dealing with difficulties, and he said something like this: "Somebody has to do something, and it's just incredibly pathetic that it has to be us."

Author: That's funny and true at the same time.

Editor: Yes, and I realized that I could continue to apply useless effort trying to change what was happening, or I could change myself and my reaction to what was happening and figure out a course of action that might move me forward.

Author: Some people, usually our relatives, never seem to get that lesson.

Editor: Well in my family, "call Sue" seems to be a standard reaction to any adversity.

Author: How do you feel about that?

Editor: Why do I always feel like I'm in therapy when I talk to you? Let me see what you have to say in this chapter about embracing adversity.

Author: I did use the word feel properly.

Editor: I noticed.

EMBRACE ADVERSITY

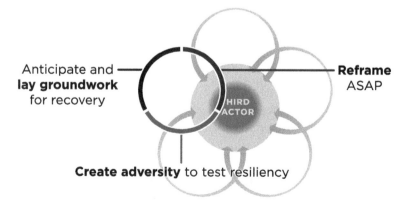

D r. Dabrowski firmly believed there could be no authentic growth without adversity. He believed that it was adversity—a crisis—that created the inner turmoil of emotions that eventually led to engaging the Third Factor and moving to a higher level. In Dabrowski's theory of "positive disintegration," adversity leads to the disintegration of the person's current inner milieu and the harnessing of "over-excitabilities"—a susceptibility to strong feelings, intense emotional reactions. The Third Factor eventually leads to reintegration at a higher level of moral and emotional growth.

We will be looking at a "lighter" version of the theory here, but the same fundamental self-transformation is in action. Only when you fail or are challenged do you get to discover what you have, what you don't have and how strong your own resources are. Ben Zander, conductor of the Boston Philharmonic Orchestra, points out that for teachers, success and failure are equal, and it isn't until we fail that we learn something.

There are some very good outcomes when we embrace and overcome adversity. It's a tremendous confidence builder, and the confidence built is the real thing, not the sometimes phony, imitative, "talking-like-I-might-be-able-to" kind. The good (and bad) news is that in today's world we certainly have ample occasion to deal with adversity.

In the work world, the history of the past few decades clearly indicates that change, volatility, uncertainty and other adverse conditions are here to stay. In other words, you can expect more of the same "weather" in the work world that you have already been experiencing. So why not coach and develop in others the attitudinal skills, attributes and competencies that will make them exceptional at quickly adjusting to and performing well in adverse conditions?

Two years ago in a workshop I was conducting, I asked the class to generate a list of competencies that would best help people deal effectively with change. We were discussing the fact that there are those who seem much more able to adjust and adapt when change occurs, while others are still dragging their feet weeks later. Someone suggested that one of the primary reasons coaching was emerging as the "go-to" management style was that it was so effective at dealing with situations where we don't know all the details but need to continue to perform at high levels. This person described coaching as "uncertainty management."

The world of sport is a terrific laboratory in that high pressure, continual change and uncertainty about the outcome are the order of the day—everything from severe injuries suffered by key personnel to last-minute changes, from losing streaks to bad weather. One of the coaches I interviewed about this subject put things in perspective when he said, incredulously, "What would you be doing in sport if you couldn't deal with adversity? That's what it's all about; that's the nature of the game."

On a typical training night in November prior to the Beijing Games, for example, I was working with some hurdlers when the Canadian champion pulled her hamstring while doing a simple, routine training run. And when 26-year-old downhill skier Jan Hudec was just a few hours away from signing a major endorsement deal, he crashed in a training run, broke his thumb and seriously injured his knee. Yet his comments the next day not only affirmed that he was feeling positive about the rehabilitation process but also spoke volumes about his ability to deal with adversity and his Third Factor:

"I have a pretty good track record of coming back from injuries and being able to perform well," declared the champion skier (silver medalist at the 2007 World Alpine Ski Championships). "With all the doctors that have been working with me, I have a good shot at this, so I am not too worried. I'm grateful for coming back and having such a great start to the season, and that's what will keep me motivated. I'm planning to come back stronger than ever from this."

What is adversity? Individuals have different thresholds, and what is a threat or danger to one person is a challenge to another. Genetic background and upbringing probably determine, to some extent, just how far each of us is able to go in embracing adversity, but we all can get better at it. There is no safety in inaction. Helen Keller probably said it best: "The timid are caught as quickly as the bold."

International figure-skating coach Doug Leigh and I were talking once about one of his athletes, who was having a rough go of it. The skater was experiencing a series of challenges that seemed terribly unfair—from nagging injuries to serious family matters. Doug commented, "Most of life's lessons are not friendly." At the personal level Doug knows of what he speaks, having dealt with cancer twice in his life.

Once again, what distinguishes coaches who are good at developing others is the conviction that **adversity can be the best teacher.** As we saw in the case of Gary Winckler in Chapter 1, good coaches move almost immediately into action, consciously shifting perspective, assessing and then taking action. They see adversity for what it is: another opportunity to ignite the Third Factor in their athletes.

It goes without saying that it's easy to bring effort to any endeavor when things are going smoothly and we are accomplishing whatever it is we are working on. Only when adversity rears its head, however, can we truly see how far an individual has progressed in their development. Competence is about being able to "do it" (whatever "it" may be) in the real environment, when it counts. You may strike golf balls with tremendous consistency on the driving range, but your level of competence is determined by what you do when playing competitive golf, with all the challenges that real-life circumstances present.

In the same way, you may be an excellent communicator in meetings where there is consensus and people are getting along. But you won't know how competent a communicator you truly are until you perform well under more adverse circumstances. Both sport and the workplace present us with countless opportunities to embrace adversity and to see it as the teacher and opportunity that it is.

Dealing with Adversity = Stronger Performance

I asked decathlon coach Andy Higgins about the need to embrace adversity if you are to develop others effectively. Here's what he had to say:

"That's not discussable, in that it is an *absolute* principle. No one is going to become excellent, competent or achieve mastery—any of those things—without consciously seeking to push the boundaries. And you cannot push them without running into adversity and having disappointments. The only way to move beyond them is to accept them for what they are: lessons that will give us what we need to take us to the next level. If we were capable of going to the next level, we wouldn't *have* the disappointment, setback, whatever. T.S. Eliot said, 'Only those who dare to go too far will ever discover how far they *can* go.'"

British coach Frank Dick had this to say in response to my question about the need to embrace adversity:

"Do you think you will encourage human development in our athletes by solving their problems? The truth is, that never develops people. **You only develop people by giving them the right level of challenge.** That is what coaches do.

"Do you think Lyford Christie became the fastest athlete in the world by running against slow people? You have to look at the tough situations. You have to get into the white water. You have to understand that by overcoming these things you are stronger not just for what will happen the next time you compete, but stronger for life. It is overcoming these things—the difficulties of life—that gives you the character to make sure that when you do move on, the energy is passed on to a new generation of athletes. You and I know that whatever mountains we have had to climb in the past, there will be tougher ones in the future. That's just the way it is, and you learn to have the character to go for the tougher mountains."

Success in sport and in life is all about learning to deal with and overcome obstacles and challenges. In today's fast-paced workplace, can you really afford to have people who drag their feet and become paralyzed when they encounter unexpected changes, disappointments, setbacks, failures—in other words, adversity? Of course not. But as a leader you have a role to play in developing in those under your care the skills that will allow them to embrace the adversity and turn it into the developmental opportunity it truly is. You can dramatically accelerate the development of the Third Factor in performers by helping them change their perception in adverse situations and overcome obstacles, thereby increasing their level of confidence and competence. **There are big wins to be had in helping others deal effectively with life's challenges.**

> ### How Adversity Can Save You Time . . . Really!
> The very speed of business, and indeed life, can create adversity. So can *not* coaching. Are you creating additional problems for yourself and your people by *not coaching?* Many people don't believe the old "spend time to save time" argument. "I don't have time to coach," you say. *So what are you doing with your time?* You may argue that "I ran out of time." But more likely, you "ran time out" on non-igniting activities. If you are a leader, then most of your "doing" needs to be through others. When you invest your time in developing others, you often prevent adversity, thus saving yourself time in the long run. So get out there and ignite!

The three tips that follow will help your performers successfully face—and embrace—adversity: anticipate and lay groundwork for recovery, reframe as soon as possible, and create adversity to test the resilience of your performers.

Anticipate and Lay Groundwork for Recovery

This one definitely isn't "rocket surgery," as the kids say. Planning to reduce the impact of adversity is an obvious course of action. But is it effective? To clarify, here's what anticipating *isn't*: it isn't expecting failure, it isn't talking to the performer about all potential disasters, and it isn't setting low standards.

It *is* about anticipating what obstacles might arise and coming up with a plan to deal with them. Tremendous confidence comes from having a plan. Adversity is a way to test that plan and further build the performer's (and coach's) confidence.

An experienced coach has a pretty good idea of all the possible pitfalls and traps the performer might fall into, and it's the coach's job to ensure that the performer has thought about these and is equipped to deal with them. I continually ask athletes what they plan to do if this, or that, or the other thing occurs. Which doesn't mean the worst will happen. (Nor does it mean they will follow the plan and avoid the adversity!)

Prior to the 1987 world figure-skating championships in Cincinnati, Ohio, I got a call from Michael Jiranek, Kurt Browning's coach, saying he couldn't be in Cincinnati for Kurt's first practice and would I look out for him. I stood at the boards with Rosemary Marks, the team leader, during Kurt's first practice. Kurt had a plan to warm up slowly and not get distracted by the exceptional group of skaters on the ice with him at the time, including Brian Boitano, then current world champion, and Brian Orser.

Someone had decided it would be a good idea to sell tickets for the practice, so there were some 15,000 spectators oohing and aahing at every jump. Rosemary and I saw very little of Kurt in the first 20 minutes as he tried to out-jump everyone on the ice. He came by for drinking water once, looking fairly exhausted, and left the ice a bit before the end of the 40-minute practice. As we were walking down the hall to the locker room, Kurt said to me, "I just did everything I vowed I would never do in my first practice at world's!"

By acknowledging this, he demonstrated great awareness and a perspective that quickly led to recovery, because he still had a workable plan and he knew what he wanted to do. He had just been blown off course by the crowd and by his own desire to please them, but he was already on the road to recovery.

So the coach's first line of action is to try to anticipate all the problems that might arise, and to help the performer develop a strategy for dealing with them—if they happen. Adversity usually occurs when the performer doesn't perform up to par or, worse, has a devastating experience—as gold-medal favorite Perdita Felicien did when she fell right out of the blocks in her race at the 2004 Olympics (described in Chapter 1).

Good coaches/leaders are always playing the "what if" game: What if my best performer gets hurt, what will I do? How will I talk to the team and what, specifically, will I say? What will my strategic response be in terms of deployment of resources? What if the plant remains closed past the expected retrofit time frame? Suppose we get off plan by 5 percent in the next quarter, what options do I have? How will I talk about it to the team in a constructive way to help with the second-quarter recovery?

You don't want your people to fail. You don't want to create a high-stress reactive environment. **You want your people to be able to handle adversity effectively and be resilient in the face of it.** You need to coach to those expectations. No golfer wants to be in the sand trap, but the good ones anticipate and prepare for that possibility.

Mel Davidson, who coached Canada's gold-medal-winning women's Olympic hockey team, told me, "I really think that if you're prepared going in, the adversity is easy to handle. If you can focus on how it's affecting everyone, then it can be advantageous, but if you are not prepared going into an event or competition, or even in practice sometimes, then your reaction is usually poor and you don't handle it well and it isn't a learning experience, it isn't a growth experience.

"At Hockey Canada, CEO Bob Nicholson, under whose tutelage I basically grew up, is a firm believer in dealing with adversity. I remember going to events and something would happen and I would think to myself, 'Bob did this, Bob did this! Things were going smoothly and he sent this so we would have some adversity!'" Bob also ignited Mel's Third Factor by helping her begin to self-direct her own growth as a coach in a very male-dominated world: ice hockey. It's no accident that she was one of the few women ever to coach Junior A men's hockey!

Hold a Broad Perspective

Perspective is critical to success in stressful or crisis situations. Just as location, location, and location are the three keys in real estate, the three essentials in the coaching process, for both leader and prodigy, are perspective, perspective, and perspective—especially in times of adversity. The leader's primary functions are to maintain a developmental perspective and to uncover and, if necessary, tweak the perspective of the performer.

I asked Andy Higgins what role he, as a coach, takes in helping his athletes deal with adversity.

"To me that's the only role a coach has. Everything else can be done by a trainer. Trainers prepare and carry out programs; coaches deal with the human being, and all the things I already talked about—setting it up early on, knowing where the real work has to be done, developing the awareness—that's the coach's job. The coach's job is to support awareness for starters because the awareness will prevent some of the difficulties from arising in the first place.

"The next question is, what do we do when we come up against a difficulty? One of my corporate clients had to declare personal bankruptcy.

I called him and asked, 'Neal, why haven't you called me?'

"He said, 'Why haven't I called you? I owe you money. It's embarrassing.'

"I said, 'Neal, you didn't hear me. I said why didn't you call me, not where is my money. You don't need me when things are going well. You're in the deepest hole of your life now. *Now* is when you need me.'

"That's really when a coach is of value, when someone is facing a difficulty—large or small. My job is to support the development of the person who is performing the skill, whether it's selling insurance or something silly like jumping these hurdles."

Being a leader, you need to reinforce the bigger picture for those under your care, continually reminding them to focus on two things: what is happening now, and their overall self-image. Sometimes the most helpful thing you can do is to remind them, at critical moments, of all that they are. In a high-pressure situation it's not unusual for every one of us to lose perspective on our capabilities and competencies. It's helpful to be reminded of all that we have dealt with and overcome in the past—problems that we may at the time have thought insurmountable—and to realize what an arsenal of skills we possess. Recalling this is empowering and truly ignites the Third Factor.

There is a wonderful Zen perspective exercise that many masters employ with their students. In the middle of a large piece of paper the master draws a small, V-like figure. He then asks the students, "What is this?"

The students respond with various ideas, from a bird to a wave. The master points out that it may indeed be a bird or a wave, but then broadens their perspective. He shows them that they have become so focused on the foreground that they have missed the background and therefore the "all" of it. If it is a bird, then it is a bird in a huge sky. If it is a wave, then it is a wave in a huge ocean.

In times of adversity it's easy to get caught up in the foreground, in what is happening now, and to forget the big picture both in terms of the end goal—what you are trying to achieve—and your own competencies and capabilities—your own Third Factor.

Your job as coach is to direct the attention of others to what is most important—to those aspects of the situation that can be controlled and where action might matter. Situation mastery is about acting where you can make a difference and letting go where you cannot. It's all too easy for some performers to give up in the face of hardship, and that can be a challenge for any leader. But the tougher issue to deal with is ceaseless striving—trying to change what cannot be changed, applying effort where no amount of effort will matter. We deal with this later, in the section on reframing.

One can misrepresent or misinterpret the directive to "anticipate and lay the groundwork for recovery." Does this mean you should go into a situation expecting the performers to fail? Do you make statements like "Look, don't expect too much from yourself" or "Don't worry if you're not successful or fail completely"? Of course not. Keep in mind that what you are trying to do is build a strong, independent performer. So pre-event conversations should encourage them to develop their Third Factor, while at the same time allowing you both to lay the groundwork for recovery in case something goes awry.

You can't debrief any performance properly unless you know what the performer was trying to accomplish in the first place. I often ask questions like "What are you hoping to accomplish? What's your strategy or plan? What's an outcome you could live with, one that would be very good, and one that would be unbelievable?" I recently put that last question to an 800 meter runner I was working with whose first indoor meet in which she was running a 600 meter race was coming up that weekend. I asked her to give me a time for 600 meters that she could live with, and she said 1:29. Her very good time would be 1:28.5, and an unbelievable time would be 1:27.5. I told her that when we debriefed after her race on Saturday, I would refer back to those times. What was the purpose of doing that? People often change their expectations and thus create their own adversity. So if she were to run, let's say, 1:28.8 and place last in the race, I now had concrete times I could remind her of during the debriefing—ones that she herself had laid out as criteria for success.

On joint sales calls, the manager needs to ask questions ahead of time related to call objective, strategy and plan, so that if a disaster does occur, there is a frame of reference for later discussion. As a leader you too want to think ahead to the possible outcomes and how you will deal with them in a developmental way. Your self-management as a leader is especially critical when performance results are at either extreme—a huge success or a devastating failure. It's hard to be developmental when you are caught up in your own reactions.

Anticipating and preparing the groundwork for recovery has to do with what your performers attribute the failure to. After a tough quarter or year, you want to make sure that the people in your department or work unit clearly understand the reasons for the disappointing results—all the contributing factors. After the analysis, they also should be able to see a course of action, a way to recover. **You really need to paint a believable picture of recovery**.

As a leader, when you anticipate the possibilities you can also work in advance to lessen the psychological blow on the performer and start the re-engagement of Third Factor in team members much sooner. In most environments today, big surprises can be kept to a minimum if you can see things coming. An authentic leader won't panic but will simply point out the obvious: "We are not going to hit our numbers because of A, B and C. What opportunities do people see here?"

Coach Gary Winckler told me about pushing Perdita Felicien around the Olympic Village in a wheelchair the evening of her Olympic disaster in 2004, thus starting right away to help her process what had taken place. I commented that in a situation like that it is always helpful to begin the process with the performer immediately in order to intervene in a possible downward spiral.

"That's so true," he said. "You want to blame someone, you want to blame *something*. The evening after it happened I hadn't had any time to look at a video and couldn't tell her exactly what had happened. The next day I looked at video for hours, from all different angles, and I still couldn't tell what had happened. As I was telling a reporter the other day, it was just one of those things that happens. Every hurdler is like every bull rider; you know you're going to fall, you know you are going to trip up at some time; it's inevitable. That's the risk you take in doing the event the way it's supposed to be done. I tell my hurdlers, 'When you feel like you are on the edge of being out of control, that's when you are running your best. You have to accept that and be cognizant of it. One of the things you have to do is not fight it, to go with the flow, like you're running down the hill, over hurdles in the dark. You know where they are; you just have to continue to go with the flow. As soon as you start to get scared and back up and fight that flow, that's when you are going to go down.'"

I said to Gary, "You took an active role with Perdita in dealing with her adversity."

"Well, you come out the next morning, and every media guy in the world is going to ask her what happened and how it happened, and four years later she'll have to go back and have this discussion again, because it's going to start all over again [in the Beijing Olympics]. Overcoming adversity is what sport is about.

"I had another athlete, Tonya Buford Bailey, who broke the world record in the world championship race in 1995 and still placed second—by 100th of a second. You cry one minute, you're laughing the next. She always had the greatest attitude: 'I know I'm going to lose more than I win,' she said. That's a pretty healthy attitude when you're willing to

---

"The Universe Works in Wonderful Ways!"

Here's an example of how coach Andy Higgins anticipates and lays the groundwork for recovery with his decathletes. He sent the following e-mail about an upcoming meet not just to his athletes but to all of us who deal with those athletes. His message is full of elements for igniting the Third Factor in others.

"The universe works in wonderful ways! This morning I came across some material on Alfred Hitchcock, the Grandfather (Godfather?) of all horror/thriller directors. Last evening Peter Jensen spoke to you about creating your own script. Hitchcock said, 'Working on the script is the real making of the film for me. When I've done it, the film is finished already in my mind.'

"'Finished already in your mind' is a great description of the ideal decathlon—the absolute best of which you are capable. Two days of being completely in control of your life and your talent. A clear culmination of the training and all the mental/emotional work you have done. Thought out and planned and scripted to the last detail.

"And when the script is clear and the work has been done, there is nothing left to do but enjoy being the lead in one terrific scene after another. Remember, this is 'sport.' At the highest level it is called the Olympic 'Games.' At the immediate and very local level, this Friday and Saturday it is called the Track Classic, which does not translate into 'deadly serious, my-worth-as-a-human-being-on-the-line test.' Peter said it last evening: 'This is the greatest life laboratory there is.' This is life in microcosm, with no real significant price to pay for mistakes and errors—unlike real life! Here you get to make mistakes and extract the lessons, and the cost is negligible. Go for it! Err and learn and get better.

"I suggested to an athlete that we are here for no other reason than to learn and improve. If any of us is already perfect at what we do and in our ability to execute it when it counts, go home and rest until the biggest meet in your life! If not, then accept the reality that everything we do is a learning opportunity, and treat it like that.

"This weekend is a big competition! 'Big' in that it is a significant learning opportunity. For each of you there is a meet this year that has real significance for you. Everything up until those two days is preparation for those two days. The more you can learn and change and improve, the more satisfaction you will derive. It's that simple. And if you really 'want it badly,' 'can taste it,' and all those other sport clichés, then start to enjoy the process, relish every day, and look for the pleasure in effort.

"Remember this: whenever it is all over for you and you move to another phase of your life, the only thing of value you take with you from these years is Who You Are!

"And you are writing the script and directing the action. The beauty in a decathlon is that there are no re-takes. This movie is shot live—one take. Love it!

"Yours in Success,

"Andy"

Sometimes I am thankful I'm helping others deal with adversities because it reminds me of the bigger picture and what matters, of all those things I also need to do! It helps me recognize that at times I need to ignite my own Third Factor and redirect myself.

accept that fact, but it doesn't detract from what you are trying to do. You are very fortunate if you ever reach a point in your career where you win more than you lose."

Reframe ASAP

Anyone who has ever framed a picture or a painting knows that when you change the colour or style of the frame, the picture looks different. The picture doesn't change, but a blue frame and matte will highlight the shades of blue in the picture, whereas a black matte and frame show up the darker colours. Similarly, life may determine events and outcomes, but the choice of frame is ours. We can consciously select the frame that highlights the developmental opportunity rather than the obstacle or setback.

During the deregulation of the telephone industry in the 1980s, Suzanne Kobasa and Salvador Maddi, two researchers from the University of Chicago, conducted an interesting seven-year study with 200 middle managers of the Illinois Bell telephone company. They studied these executives as they went through turbulent changes in their industry, staying in constant communication with them and performing annual medicals on them. At the end of the study it was clear that some of the managers had thrived while others had not. Of those who had failed to thrive, one of the major indicators was a rate of absenteeism from work due to illness six to seven times higher than among those who had successfully withstood the stress. In examining the differences between the two groups, Kobasa and Maddi discovered that there were three main resistance resources that allowed people to stay healthy and perform at high levels: personality hardiness, exercise and strong social support.

The likelihood of illness developing in stressed executives was 93 percent if no resistance resources were present, but less than 8 percent if all three resistance resources were present—a colossal difference, to put it mildly. Exercise and strong social support had what the researchers called a small buffering effect. This is understandable. Exercise may help to reduce the stress, but you still have to go into the work environment every day, and strong social support would soon start to decline—in my house anyway!—if I continued to come home complaining about my job for seven years.

The factor that most strongly influenced the health of the executives was *personality hardiness*. These people optimistically appraised events and took the decisive actions that would alter them. They did this by embracing the three *C*s: commitment, control and challenge. They chose to see what they were going through as interesting and important (commitment), capable of being influenced (control), and of potential value for personal development (challenge). What they were doing, of course, was *reframing*: choosing to take a perspective of events that would help them move forward. This action-oriented perspective activates the Third Factor, helping people move from "what is" to "what ought to be."

It's All About That Conversation

Synchronized swimming coach Debbie Muir outlined the role she takes in helping her athletes deal with adversity, failure and the unexpected.

"It's all about having that conversation. I remember when we were in Seoul in June before the September Olympics, and we actually lost. The first time since '84 that [gold medalist] Carolyn [Waldo] lost . . . I remember before the meet we ran into *Toronto Star* reporter Randy Starkman.

"'How important is it that you win here?' he asked.

"'Oh, really important' I said. 'We have to win this because the judges are going to use this going into the Olympics as a preconceived idea of who is the best, so our goal is to win this pre-Olympics meet.' And then we lost.

"Then he came back and said 'You know, three days ago you told me it was most important to win this and you didn't, so what do you think now?'

"'Well, you know, it's really important that we lost because if we hadn't, we would go into the Olympics thinking we were the greatest,' I said. After the loss I remember Carolyn went to her room (she wouldn't cry in public) and had a huge meltdown. When that was over and she came out, we said, 'Okay, what are we going to do about this, what's the lesson? What have we become complacent about, what do we need to do differently, what have we done really well?' You can't ignore that or take too long to get over it . . . "

Modes of Reframing

The method of reframing that you use and how you use it will depend on the nature of the situation you are faced with and what you or the group most needs. There are times, for example, when you need to find the energy to tackle a difficult change. At those times what the group may need most is the energy just to begin the process. Often, sitting down and brainstorming what the opportunities are in dealing with this issue is the first step. Perhaps you ask the question "What would be the benefits if we dealt effectively with this issue?" When you see what you might gain, you usually see the upside to handling an issue effectively, and that enables you to find the energy to deal with it.

A second mode of reframing is to sit down with the person or team and, as a first step, let them "awfulize" about it, to use a term coined by psychologist Joan Borysenko. You might ask, for example, in a situation where significant change is required or is already taking place, "What are the dangers in going through this change, in making this transition?" Allow people to list all the inherent dangers. If you're an optimist, this tactic might be a little hard on you. Optimists hate to hear all the negative stuff. But don't stop the process—just let it all come out. Then start at the top of the list and work on each item, deciding which you have control over and which you don't (and therefore need to let go of). Of those you have control over, you can now ask the three questions from the hardiness study: "What aspects of this do I have control over?" "Is there anything I can see as a challenge for personal growth and development?" "Is there anything here that I can commit to?" **It is always surprising in any situation to discover how many possibilities there are for action.** This discovery recharges and re-engages the Third Factor in those involved.

A third method of reframing is simply to say to the group or the individual something like "We don't want to go through this and we don't like having to go through it, but seeing as we have no choice, where are the opportunities?" Taking a situation that you're faced with and making a decision to look for the opportunities is the simplest and most direct way of reframing.

Victor Frankel, in his landmark book *Man's Search for Meaning*, pointed out that the one thing that can never be taken from us is our attitude toward a situation. He called perspective "the last human freedom." Because of his own experience he believed that meaning saved lives in the German concentration camps; that given the chance, those who were somehow able to create a sense of purpose and meaning out of what they were going through were the ones most likely to survive. Extreme though this example is, it does make the point: life may choose what we have to deal with, but *we* choose the perspective we take. Frankel's book is in line with Dabrowski's theory about the Third Factor; it is about moral and emotional growth in the darkest of times.

The sooner we start the act of reframing, the better. Immediacy is important for all post-performance discussions. Coach Gary Winckler makes it clear that he wants to talk to his athletes about their performance right after an event, no matter how it went.

"I tell every athlete after a performance that I want them to come and talk to me. Whether it's just a small competition or a major event, we will talk about what happened. We will analyze what went well and what went wrong. We'll talk about how we can fix it—and then we're going to forget, we're going to move on—take the things we need to work on and move on. That's probably adversity at its lowest grade, just figuring out how to move forward and not dwelling on what happened in the past. If I take a video of the race and it's a disaster, the video is never seen by the athlete. It's just never looked at again. You can't learn anything from it. Every day in training, your attitude has to be 'I'm going to learn something from competition and I'm going to try to use that information to make the next time I do this a better experience.'"

Reframing is also a great team/group skill. I once worked with a group of leaders in Tulsa, Oklahoma, who were faced with the challenging task of helping their people through a difficult transition. The more than 600 employees in this organization had no idea if they would have a job three months down the road. Their organization, a large oil company, was merging with an even larger one, and it was clear that the culture of the larger company would become the dominant one. The employees didn't know whether they would receive a buy-out, see the company sold out from under them, end up in a new, separate company selling their services back to the merged organization, or simply stay on as employees in the new company.

I spent a day talking with the leaders about how they might assist their people at this difficult time. We spoke of many things, including reframing. The reframing took the form of a facilitated exercise in which the leader drew a line down the center of a flip-chart page and on the left-hand side encouraged the group to generate a list of all the dangers inherent in their current position. People were encouraged to "awfu-lize." I reminded the more optimistic of the leaders not to cut this list short—optimists often want to jump to a solution too quickly. Once the employees had exhausted all possibilities for this list, I encouraged them to go to the blank, right-hand side, and, taking each item on the left side, to generate a list of possibilities from the three Cs in the hardiness study: control, challenge and commitment.

They addressed each item with questions based on those three Cs: "Is there anything here over which we have control?" "Is there any aspect of this that I can see as a challenge?" "In relation to this item, is there anything I can commit to doing?" It wasn't long before they started to see some possibilities they could begin to act on. Now, I am in no way suggesting that these opportunities were preferable to not experiencing crisis. But when you *are* in a crisis you might as well figure out where you can best act and where you need to let go, so that you can ignite the group's Third Factor and start them on the road to what is possible.

Winners or Losers? Time Will Tell

A few weeks before Christmas quite a few years ago, I did a workshop for a food company. Of the just over 100 people in the room, 51 knew they were going to lose their job with the organization in the next three months. One of the things I pointed out that day was that we would not know who the "winners" and the "losers" in the room were until two or three years down the road. I also pointed out that the outcome would have nothing whatsoever to do with whether they were staying with the organization or leaving it. Within three years of conducting that seminar, I was hired on two separate occasions by people who had left the organization and had found great success elsewhere.

Create Adversity to Test Performers' Resilience

The most effective way to build confidence in our performers is through the successful completion of a challenging goal, or through the triumphant conquering of adversity. Genuine confidence, real confidence, comes from the successful completion of a task important to the performer. We may praise them and rain accolades on them, but when it comes to developing authentic confidence, accolades pale in comparison with achievement.

This is one of the reasons coaches focus on performance goals and not end goals. Competence is best developed through a series of successes in the real game, at the real task. And as a leader you can also learn a lot about the "reach" of your performers when they are performing under a bit of pressure that you have created in order to develop them fully. There is an old Buddhist expression, "Every meditation hall needs a fly." Sometimes you need to create adversity or a challenge to be able to determine how far the performer has developed, and to prepare them for the fact that very soon these timelines, this pace, these high numbers will be commonplace.

I want to point out that **creating adversity is not about being mean, it is about being developmental.** We have to assist people in moving out of their comfort zone if we're going to develop them. We owe it to them to prepare them for what we know is coming. The leaders at NASA, for example, put potential astronauts through numerous simulations in order to develop them adequately for future missions. In my work in sport I have organized many simulations to prepare athletes for the adversity of competing in the Olympic arena. What follows are four examples from the world of sport, and then a look at how this concept might ignite the Third Factor of those in the workplace.

Prior to the 2006 Torino Olympics, the Canadian Women's Olympic hockey team was playing an exhibition game against Sweden in Calgary. These two teams would eventually meet in the gold-medal game in Torino. The Canadian team was down 2–0 at the end of the first period, a position they had never been in before in any game with Sweden. I expected Canadian coach Mel Davidson to be upset with the level of play, but she was almost giddy as she entered the coaches' room. Rubbing her hands together she said, "All right, this is new for them. Let's see how they handle it!"

On another occasion I asked British coach Frank Dick, "Did you ever create adversity to test athletes?"

"Oh sure, in a very amateur way. Noises when athletes were running up to do, for example, the long jump. When they only had one jump left in the evening . . . noise of a crowd, music, a starter's pistol.

"Ian Robertson, who was under my wing as a young lad in Scotland, was coaching two Scottish girls who were going to New Zealand to compete at the Commonwealth Games. Neither had been in a major stadium. Competing in the west of Scotland championships is rather different from a World Games arena. So he set up a deal with the Celtic football club: the girls jogged around the perimeter of the track at half-time and were introduced: 'These are our girls going to represent Scotland.' And the crowd roared and both girls came off the track trembling, absolutely trembling. That was a clever move."

I also asked Gary Winckler if he trained for adversity with his athletes.

"Yes, constantly. In hurdling, for example, the way I approach the event is that you want to reach this state of abandonment. It's not a run over 10 hurdles; it's 11 accelerations, trying to get faster each time. When the athlete gets comfortable with a certain spacing of the hurdles, then what I do is maybe put the hurdles closer together to force some things to happen that might happen in a competition. Or we will race with a really big tailwind behind us, where we have to deal with higher velocities than we've dealt with before. As you do that, you create problems. You create problems with the takeoff, you create problems with the steps between the hurdles—and it forces the athlete to learn how to adapt to those situations. We spend a lot of time creating adversity in order to get the training effect. You could say it's just a simple application of the principle of overload. When we try to get an athlete stronger, we increase the overload, make it more difficult. We present the adversity to the training."

David Hemery, coach and gold-medal hurdler, said he, too, plans for adversity.

"When I was out doing hill reps in the winter with this not-quite-17-year-old, he agreed to do two sets of four. They were about 200 meters long. After the sixth one he felt rubbery, after the seventh he threw up and was on his hands and knees. And I thought: 'I was in my 20s when I was doing this, and he's not quite 17. Do I push him?' I didn't make the decision for him. I asked him, 'Do you want to walk around a little longer?' And he said, 'Yes, I do.' I said, 'Do you want to go back down to the bottom, back at the start, and decide when you would want to go?' And he said, 'Yes.' We went down to the bottom and he took a good two or three minutes' extra rest and then did a personal best on the eighth one, then threw up again, really in bad shape. And I just said, 'I am truly proud of you, but I hope you're more proud of yourself. You worked there to earn your time next summer. You'll never have to run that hard and dig that deep in a race, but the fact that you've been there means that in a race, when it gets tough you will be able to hang on while hurting. You have just earned yourself the times you want to run this summer.'"

So how might you apply this concept to performers in the work world? We put the question to a group of business leaders at two of our seminars. The first story is a good example of how *not* to do it!

Shaking the tree. One manager talked about a company with which he had previously worked. There was a change in management, and the new manager who took over his department decided he was going to find out what his new team was capable of, through a process he called "shaking the tree." Essentially this involved piling on the work, giving his people really challenging goals and tough assignments to see who sank and who learned how to swim and swim well—but providing them with very little guidance or support. The problem is that if you shake the tree too hard, you dislodge not only the bad apples, but a lot of the good ones as well. And unlike apples, people have the inclination and the ability to move to a more stable tree. So, while this process did help that manager quickly assess who his best people were, many of those were the first ones to walk out the door—highly sought after, they were capable of landing jobs with other organizations. On top of that, to this day that organization has an underground reputation of being a "hellish place to work," and has a tough time recruiting new talent.

The rich get richer. One manager described how the best boss she ever had used to reward his good people by giving them increasingly tougher assignments. But although the difficulty of the assignments did require more time spent on planning and strategizing, it wasn't a case of just piling on more work. The tougher assignments were characterized by complicated situations, with more legal, policy and administrative restrictions, greater technical and logistical challenges, and the involvement of more parties/departments/interest groups—in other words, it was really interesting work.

His people loved it. These assignments gave them a chance to hone their skills and develop reputations as "A Players." They gave these employees increased visibility inside and outside the organization, and created a culture of achievement within his department. After doing this for a while, he noticed two highly desirable but quite unexpected results. First, good people sought out his department, which had developed a reputation as a place to go if you were really smart and motivated and wanted to improve your skills for the next level. Second, his people were, as he put it, nearly "immune to the consequences of change." Because they were used to seeing the value in taking on new and challenging tasks, and because they were good at putting together and executing strategies under such circumstances, organizational change had become routine stuff for them.

Shift in perspective. One sales manager with an office technology company described how his boss used to help top salespeople make the transition from selling to managing. The challenge this manager faced was that, traditionally, people in sales roles get promoted to sales manager because they are skilled at selling. They know it, and they have been recognized and rewarded for it throughout their career. The tendency therefore is for newly promoted sales managers to "do it yourself" or micromanage the sales staff, behavior they see as being "helpful" or "supportive."

What this boss did was start piling on the work while staying around and observing the new sales manager closely. These deliberately chosen assignments were ones that could be done by the sales staff but were complicated enough to tempt the new sales manager to take them on instead. After the work volume reached a certain point, the boss would notice signs of overload (longer hours in the office, work taken home, symptoms of stress, lack of visibility outside their office, impatience, slipping deadlines, etc.). That's when he would have what was known as "the talk," which essentially went something like this:

"You have unbelievable sales skills, and for many years you have added tremendous value to the organization through using those skills to move our product. That is no longer your role. Your role is to develop, guide and support your team of hired guns to go out there and sell. I have noticed that you seem to be working a lot of late nights. I know I've been sending a ton of work your way. My expectation is not that you will do this work yourself, but that you will hand it off to your people and that you will prepare them, guide them and support them so they are capable of getting it done. So let's sit down, take a look at the assignments on your plate, assess where your team is at, and see who might be capable of taking on some of them."

Why did this manager of sales managers take this approach? It was his experience that until you let people struggle a bit—create some adversity for them—they don't know that what they are currently doing won't work in the long term. The realization opens them up to new options.

Three weeks in spring. One sales manager with a communications firm developed a routine that she put in place with her sales teams going into the summer months. Her view was that the summer months, particularly in Canada, were for enjoying the fine weather and spending time with family, and she wanted to make sure her people developed good work routines so that the work did not expand to fill up their free time. In the second week of April, she required that they work no more than a 40-hour week; in the second week of May, no more than 35 hours. And during the second week in June (when there were always many social events and school-related commitments), they were to try to meet their targets working a 30-hour week. At the end of each week they would share with each other systems, processes and tricks that they had found helped them to get the work done in the time allotted.

In her mind this achieved several major goals. First, it really drove home to her people the point that she expected them to enjoy a life outside of work. Second, it created an environment where people were challenged and excited to think about being more efficient—but with the goal of having more time for themselves, not just to get more done for the company. And finally, she found that when they really had periods of challenging targets to meet, the lessons of the three weeks in spring provided useful skills and systems that helped them.

Growing while giving back. One sales manager with a high-tech company used charitable endeavors as an opportunity to expose his people to adversity and grow the capabilities of his team. Each year the team chose a special project that would significantly benefit the lives of people much less fortunate. Then, based upon the chosen target, they would put in place a challenging goal. In each case, the sales manager would push the team to set a really audacious goal, one in which the chance of failure was estimated to be at least 30 to 40 percent. There were only a few rules attached to this endeavor. First, it had to be a new cause each time. Second, the role of spearheading the effort had to rotate among individuals each year. Third, there were guidelines/limits for how much they were expected to contribute personally in hours and funds.

If the team reached its goal, they would have a celebration party. If they failed, they would have a "wake." In either case this took the form of a family barbecue hosted by the sales manager at his house, where he provided all the food and drink, and he and his wife and kids cooked and served the guests.

He found that this charitable endeavor provided a safe environment for his team to challenge their abilities, work together as a team and try out new roles (project leadership, planning/strategy, finances, marketing/communication). The fact that it was a new project each year helped keep things fresh and forced people to be creative and not just work off past templates. It also encouraged dialogue as they tapped into the expertise of the people who had had their roles the previous year. The added bonuses for all this effort were a contribution to a worthy cause, an opportunity to celebrate together, and a sense of perspective about what was really important.

Confrontation = Creating Adversity

There will be times when you have a change you want a performer to make and you have tried questioning, feedback and the other, more collaborative communication skills, but the person is still not engaged in the desired behavior or at the required performance level. When this happens, you will need to move into a more confronting style of communication. The act of confronting can create adversity for both the recipient and the leader, but it will occasionally be necessary if you are to ignite the Third Factor in them.

You have to be careful not to confront in a manner that is so personal that it shuts the person down. The individual needs to be able to move from being upset with *you,* or with what you are pointing out, to a more internalized realization and acknowledgment that they are not rising to this particular challenge or change. As coach or leader, you need to make sure the "failure" is attributed to something over which the other person has control and can change—through increased effort, for example, a shift in perspective, a newly perceived chance to learn, or a willingness to risk trying and "failing."

Positioning the issue as a developmental opportunity is far more helpful than focusing on it as "a major problem" (except in the fairly infrequent circumstances where this is really called for). And making your expectations clear ("I know you can do this") reinforces the message that a positive outcome is achievable. If you position any conflict in a developmental way you will engage the Third Factor in the other person and increase their motivation to be "more like this" (a future state) and "less like now" (the present state). For those who really want to delve into the "how-tos" of confronting, Appendix B includes a detailed map for this challenging process.

Extinguishers generally react poorly in times of adversity.
- They don't see it coming or put blinders on, hoping it won't come—and therefore prepare no one, least of all themselves.
- They are into blaming, not reframing.
- They create lots of adversity—but not for any developmental reasons!

To be an Igniter remember this!
- Anticipate and lay the groundwork for recovery.
- Reframe ASAP.
- Create adversity to test the resilience of your performers.

Editor: I really liked what that coach had to say. The one who said that if we had what it took to do it or move to the next level, we wouldn't have the setback or adversity in the first place.

Author: Andy Higgins.

Editor: Yeah. But it's sure irritating when it first happens. It's not like I instantly reframe.

Author: That reminds me of a meeting I had once with a figure skater named Ben Ferreira. I was reviewing with him a self-assessment he had written. At those times it's sometimes difficult to hear about shortcomings or personal challenges and not get defensive. He did his best to be open to his results, then accurately captured the moment by saying to me, "The truth will set you free, but first it will piss you off!"

Editor: I couldn't have said it better! I really think this will help me with my children.

Author: I get so many questions from business leaders about their children during workshop breaks. It's amazing. I am doing a corporate training event and they are asking me about their teenagers!

Editor: Doesn't surprise me in the least. I face numerous challenges in my managing at work, but they pale in comparison with the importance of what I do at home with my family. There is also a lot of angst attached to parenting. I want to do it right. It can be very draining, and I don't want to fail or feel like a failure. I want to have a wonderful lifelong relationship with my children. That's very important to me.

Author: Yeah, I know the feeling. I really wanted to make more reference to "parent as developer" throughout Ignite the Third Factor, *but I think it would have brought too much confusion to the book.*

Editor: You're right, but what about a section here, at the end, after this chapter?

Author: I always vowed after I had four children that I'd never, ever, give advice on parenting.

Editor: Think of it as developmental advice to those of us who are not only leaders but also happen to have children.

Author: I'll give it a shot, but it will be brief—unless I can get Sandra to help me.

Editor: Now there's an idea! Bring in a credible source.

Author: You just had to get one last shot in, didn't you.

Editor: Aaww, you know I didn't mean it.

8

Where Igniting the
Third Factor Matters Most
— At Home

Author: So here we are at your chapter on parenting. I still think it's a bit weird to have a chapter on parenting in a business book.

Editor: Whatever happened to your "doing something new or different" philosophy from the opening chapter?

Author: It's just that, I don't know . . . talking about parenting is not really done in business.

Editor: Hold it right there. In my business we talk about it all the time . . . well, at breaks, lunch, et cetera. Someone is always asking for advice, help, feedback. It's the toughest job we do—and the most important.

Author: It is. Someone once said that if we could raise one generation of children "properly," 90 percent of the world's problems would disappear.

Editor: So we break with convention and add a chapter here. I am sorry this is creating adversity for you. Can you imagine yourself doing this? How can I help you over this block? You may have to manage your tendency to react and broaden your belief about what is possible.

Author: Okay, stop, I get it. Let's get started.

Editor: You will note from my comments that I have been paying attention to what you have written so far.

Author: Duly noted.

This chapter focuses on the five areas outlined in this book—Manage Yourself, Build Trust, Encourage and Use Imagery, Uncover and Work Through Blocks, and Embrace Adversity—as they apply to the challenging but rewarding task of raising children. Those of you who are parents may find it especially interesting to look at how each of the five areas can be applied to the parenting role.

First, a few general thoughts, in no particular order:

I believe we **parents ought to talk about the Third Factor to our children as soon as they can grasp the concept.** It gives them a "handle" on their role, a solid way of thinking about their involvement in their own development.

Talk to your children about the role of disquietude, or even outright conflict, in development. It almost always takes a crisis or some form of discomfort to promote evolution to a new level in any endeavor. Understanding this helps children to reframe what they are going through. You may need to give them some time, a breather, before you head into reframing. All of us need time to mourn or vent in dealing with losses, changes, hardships, et cetera.

Get comfortable using phrases such as "moving from what is to what ought to be" and "sorting out what feels more like yourself from what feels less like yourself." Talk to your partner about your child's over-excitabilities and how these strong feelings and emotional reactions might inform the two of you about your parenting approach.

Talk to your children about their emotions and over-excitabilities as they arise and cause dissonance for them: "Yes, you feel strongly, imagine vividly, think deeply—what a gift!" Ask questions and follow up with some ideas on how they might channel those feelings into something developmental. Children with excitabilities are often told they are "too"—as in *too* emotional, *too* touchy, *too* imaginative, *too* smart for their own good. They need to know that it's okay to feel this way, and that they can use the energy beneath the emotion and apply it to something they need to do. (I used to say to my children, teasingly, "When you're angry you should vacuum the house!")

Intrinsic motivation is always preferable to and more powerful than extrinsic motivation. Therefore, **make sure that whatever they are do-**

ing, it is "theirs" and relates to their inner needs and satisfactions. Let them "own" it.

Ranier Martins, a sport psychologist at the University of Illinois, tells an engaging story about an old man who lived in a house on a corner lot where children from a nearby school gathered to play at the end of the school day. One day the old man went out and said to them, "I really love the fact that you come here every day and make all that wonderful noise outside my house, and I hope you'll come back and do it again tomorrow." He then gave each child 25 cents. The children made a lot of noise that day!

The next day immediately after school the children were all outside the house playing and making a lot of noise. The old man came out and said to them, "Look, I don't have as much money as I had yesterday, but I do have 10 cents for each of you as thanks for making all that noise, and I do hope you'll be back tomorrow." The children made a good deal of noise, but not quite as much as they had the day before.

The next day not as many children showed up outside the old man's house, but those who did played noisily. Once again the old man came out of his house, but this time he said to the children, "I can't give you any money today, but I do have a pop bottle for each of you that you can return for a refund as thanks for the noise you're making." The children made a bit of noise that day before moving on to other things.

I'm sure you see where this is going. The next day very few children appeared in front of the old man's house, and when he came out and told them, "I can't give you anything today, but I do hope you'll be back tomorrow," the children left, and after that they no longer played outside his house. The lesson of Ranier's story is clear. By shifting to external reward, the old man successfully regained his quiet street corner.

Be aware of what you are rewarding and reinforcing. Another story of Ranier's, about Little League baseball, makes this point well. A 10-year-old child steps to the plate in a Little League baseball game to face his 12-year-old counterpart on the mound, who has matured early and been shaving for six months. Overpowered, the younger boy watches the first two strikes before swinging feebly at the third. He walks over to the dugout, stores his bat in the bat rack and puts his helmet on the shelf. No one says anything.

Another young child steps into the batter's box with a look of determination on his face. He swings so hard at the first pitch that his helmet rotates 90 degrees on his head and he is looking out the ear-hole! Disgusted, he steps out of the batter's box and pounds his bat on the ground as his coach wanders down the third-base line and yells at him, "That's okay, Johnny, go get the next one!"

After three vicious swings that don't get him within a foot of the ball, Johnny angrily walks toward the dugout, tosses his helmet in disgust, throws his bat and flops on the bench, the picture of disappointment and frustration. His coach walks over and says, "Atta boy, Johnny, good effort, you'll get him next time!"

The coach believes he is reinforcing good effort, and that "trying hard" should be rewarded with praise. From our vantage point, however, we can see that he is also reinforcing bat and helmet throwing. As parents and coaches of young people, we need to be very careful about what we are reinforcing, and, as we learned in the feedback section, be clear and specific in what we say to them.

No matter what anyone may tell you, it is important what types of images and pictures your children watch. It's hard to believe this isn't obvious to everyone, but children are more aggressive when they watch aggressive movies. Imagery is the language of the body. I hate to be suggestive here, but think about this: Why does pornography have a physiological impact on people? It's because *images are events to the body*. It is important that you monitor what your children see. Once the images are internalized, especially in very sensitive children, they can have a negative impact for a long time, as sensitive adults will tell you.

It can be incredibly challenging to raise a child with strong feelings and emotions and a vivid imagination. Psychologist Kazimierz Dabrowski's theory in general is immensely reassuring to parents of such children. I am sure that is why, though the theory is virtually unknown in most clinical psychology circles, it is prevalent in the area of gifted education.

Manage Yourself

Many years ago, when she was in her final year of high school, my young-est daughter, Erika, asked me at the dinner table if I could take her to the store after supper for school supplies to start a new semester. "Sure," I replied. "What do you need to get?" She responded with a long list that finished with a barely mumbled item. Now as every parent knows, it's the mumbled item that is the critical one.

"What was that last thing?" I inquired. "Electronic calculator," she re-plied, hanging her head—as well she might. I had already purchased two calculators for her despite our family rule of buying only the first of any item; any others are supposed to be the responsibility of the person who wants them. I had invoked that rule a year earlier when, on a trip to the mall, Erika had requested a new calculator. "We bought the first one; you buy this one," I told her on that occasion. "Dad," she protested, "it's not fair." "Oh it's very fair," I replied. "No it isn't," she insisted, "Henry Wong took it." Henry was a classmate of Erika's who had returned with his family to Hong Kong, apparently with Erika's calculator, which, given where they are made, is like taking sand to the beach. So I gave in and bought her a new calculator.

Now, a year later, here she was saying she needed another one. I tread-ed lightly at first. My wife didn't know that I had bought the second calculator and I didn't relish having her find out that I had caved on my own rule (I am already considered the "weak link" in its application!). "I can't believe you've lost it," I said to Erika. "I didn't lose it," she replied. "It's in my backpack."

She retrieved the backpack, and indeed there it was, right at the bot-tom, where it had been cushioning heavy textbooks every time she dropped her backpack on the floor. The books were in relatively good shape; the calculator was toast.

Up until that point I had been keeping it together, but now she looked at me and said in an exasperated tone, "Dad, I don't see what the big deal is; we can always buy another one." These are only words to a 17-year-old, but to someone of my generation . . . well, the father in me vanished like smoke and out came what could best be described as a combination boxer-flamethrower.

"Buy another one!" I yelled, and off I headed into all the stuff I vowed I would never say if I ever had children. My father jumps out of my mouth, my mother jumps out of my mouth, my aunt Alma makes a guest appearance. Out come all the "*We* never had this, you just don't care" . . . all that stuff that even as I'm saying it, a part of my brain is telling me, "I can't believe you're saying this!"

As I paused for breath in the middle of this tirade, Erika gave me a look of complete and utter disgust, such as only a parent of a teenager has truly experienced. Face contorted, she yelled back, "As if! As if!" Then, with acid dripping from every word, added, "I wasn't expecting *you* to buy it. I've been saving my money from babysitting."

This was an ignominious moment for me as a parent. What had happened to me? Where had my parenting skills gone? I had totally abdicated to what the situation and her statement "we can always buy another one" triggered in me. I had no longer been in charge; my feelings and physical responses had taken over. I had displayed no developmental bias whatsoever.

Is there anywhere in life where self-control is as difficult, and as important, as during those most trying of parenting moments? I'm sure even a Zen Buddhist monk, were he a parent, would lose it on occasion with his offspring! What is it about parenting that makes self-management so difficult? I suspect we could fill a book on that topic. At any rate, it is important that you know your triggers—what throws you into a high-arousal, narrow-focus state, where your eyes bulge and your mother and father jump out of your mouth.

My trigger, in the story above, was Erika's statement "We can always buy another one." It tapped into a deep belief system concerning frugality and wastefulness that was drummed into me as a child. If you are going to parent effectively, you need to know your hot buttons. Another hot button for me was room tidiness. A messy room strewn with clothes implied, in my mind at least, a lack of respect for the work involved in providing those clothes, no understanding of the privilege and good fortune in owning them, and no empathy for less fortunate people. These, of course, were tenets of *my* belief system and had nothing whatsoever to do with my children's behavior or what was happening in the moment.

When my children were much younger, I spent a lot of time complaining, sometimes bitterly, about the state of their rooms. My wife, on the other hand, rarely let it bother her. She closed their doors and "let sleeping clothes lie." What was important to Sandra was that the clothes were off the floor on Wednesdays, when the whole house got a thorough cleaning. So, from her perspective, their rooms had to be tidied once a week. She once asked me what sort of relationship I wanted to have with the children. Did I want to sacrifice my relationship with them for a tidy room? Was this the hill I wanted to die on? Sandra felt we had bigger fish to fry.

At some point in the middle of all this I got some excellent coaching from Joan Borysenko, who wrote an amazing book, *Minding the Body, Mending the Mind.* Joan's coaching was simple and came in the form of a question: "Do you want to be right or do you want to be happy?"

What exceptional insight! I decided I wanted to be happy and began to act on it. On one occasion I got halfway into my daughter's room, noticed my face getting red, my chest tightening, my feelings of frustration and anger building, and my mind telling me what an irresponsible child I had. I spun on my heel and headed out of the room repeating to myself, "Happy. I want to be happy." (I'd love to tell you that I was able to apply Joan's coaching all the time, but I wouldn't be comfortable living with such a lie!)

It is not my intention to repeat all the information on active awareness included elsewhere in this book, but simply to remind you of a few key points. I have an abiding belief that most of us are born with all the wisdom we need to move toward our own excellence—to develop our unique potential in a way that serves the greater good. It's a matter of being able to hear that wisdom and have the trust to follow it. This requires quieting all the noise that comes from the world via the body, mind and feelings so that we can hear our own wisdom and align ourselves with that. I can think of nowhere more important to apply that wisdom than in the act of raising a child. The skills we have discussed in this book help with that process.

Body, Mind and Feelings

Your body, mind and feelings are the means through which you interact with the world. They are your personality—both what the world observes about you and the means through which you communicate who you are and how you want to connect. **They are not, however, all of who you are. You are much more than these.** This is something parents frequently forget.

The body, mind and feelings are incredibly sensitive radar, constantly informing you about the world at large and at the same time letting you know how it is impacting on you. In this way they stimulate, enrich and educate you about the world and yourself in relation to it.

It is not unusual, however, for your mind to give you way more information than you really want or need. Your mind sometimes becomes fascinated with an idea or event that isn't relevant to your life or won't move you toward how you want to behave as a parent. Your mind may tenaciously hold on to a belief system that is counterproductive to what you have to deal with right now (my example above, about room tidiness, is a case in point). Your feelings often give you information you don't want to hear or don't know how to handle. Your body often wants to do things it shouldn't do or avoid doing things it should. It can be quite a confusing jumble of sensations, images and thoughts to pay attention to!

Most of us have had very little guidance or direct coaching on how to manage all this input and still parent effectively. It really comes down to what we learned from observing how our own parents and other role models handled things. Some of us had great teachers; others weren't so lucky.

Observing what is happening within you rather than *becoming* what is happening to you is a major step in achieving the personal freedom to become the parent you want to be, and accomplishing what you want to accomplish. Then, you are no longer prisoner to the ever-changing and sometimes overpowering thoughts and feelings that can block and undermine your ongoing development as a parent.

In *observing* what is happening to you rather than *being* what is happening to you, you free yourself up to trace reactions and feelings back to their origin—to understand them, change them, redirect them. By moving to an observing role, you free up your will, your ability to choose. Rather than *being* angry and acting out of anger, you can observe that you are angry and decide how you want to respond, taking into account everything else you're facing and feeling and not losing sight of your ultimate goal as a parent in a particular situation.

This, in my opinion, is personal freedom. It is accessible to all of us, in any situation. Moving to a place of observation gives us the freedom to chart a path leading to a personally meaningful existence, and to stay on that path in spite of the sometimes distorted or distracting information coming from within ourselves, or from the world at large.

It is the daily decisions, the moment-to-moment choices you make, that determine your ability to keep on the right "parenting" path. This moment-to-moment wisdom depends on the degree to which you have developed your knowledge about your own path, what is right for you, and on your ability to recognize the distractions and distortions as they arise. It's about going through life awake. Often the distractions look like the path, or are a lot more inviting than the path you need to take. Distortions, on the other hand, are often invisible because they have been adopted as "the truth." You no longer recognize that you have adopted a belief system as if it were a truth, even when this truth may be undermining your development, your ability to adapt to a new situation, or your relationships. Nowhere is this more evident than at a minor sporting event your child is competing in!

Even back in the days when my kids were growing up I knew this stuff, yet I needed to be extremely vigilant when any of my children were engaged in a competitive activity where others were watching and, I thought, evaluating, not just the game, but, in my distorted view, how good a job I was doing as a father. These are tough moments for any parent because competition can bring out the worst in us, and we can quickly lose touch with our developmental bias. It can also be embarrassing. (Sandra has reproduced an article she wrote on parenting young athletes for the e-mail newsletter we send to our clients. You'll find it in Appendix A.)

Here is a neat little tool I use with athletes. It helps them notice what gets triggered in them so they can learn to manage themselves under pressure.

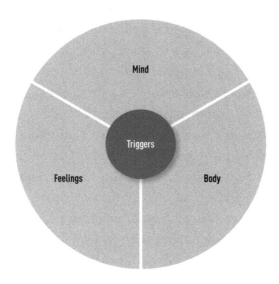

Here's the thing: **You can't manage what you aren't aware of.** It is rare indeed that we notice what triggers our impulse to react. Most often you will notice the *results* of that trigger—the sensations at the body, mind and feelings level. Stick with me here; this is important and will be clear in a minute. Think of the sensations—increased heart rate, red face, tight chest, angry, upset, disappointed or racing thoughts such as "how dare they" or "this is terrible"—as a warning light, like the "check engine" light in your car. They are telling you that things aren't right, and that you are in an emotionally reactive state, which can be very destructive. In this state a person is least human, least moral, least evolved—it's a primitive state that rarely leads to good parenting. The notable exception is in the case of an emergency, such as that of a car bearing down on your child. In that instance the high arousal/narrow focus that comes from our reaction to what is happening is useful. But most situations are not so dire—even though we may react as if they were!

Because you are human, you have not only the capacity to anticipate and prepare for potentially challenging parental moments but also the ability to manage yourself while in the midst of them. (I cover much of this in detail in Appendix B and Chapter 2: Manage Yourself.)

Here is how I have athletes and coaches use the diagram above. In the center, identify the trigger. To get you started I'll use an example from my own parenting experience:

My son has given me little information and no details about a party he wants to go to. It turns out it's been scheduled for days, but I'm asked about it at the last minute, when I get home from work on Friday night somewhat late and stressed out.

That's the trigger. Here's my reaction:

Mind: What's going on here? Am I being "played"? Why did he wait so long? Who are these kids? Is there the possibility of drugs being present? He's up to something, otherwise I would have heard about it sooner, et cetera.

Body: Heart rate up, face flushed, body language tight and closed, tension in back and chest, et cetera.

Feelings: Used, pressured, irritated, uncertain, scared, angry, et cetera.

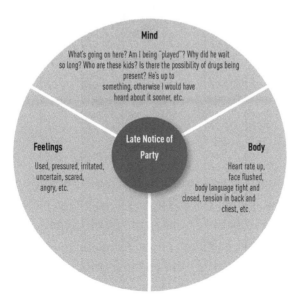

Let's stop here for a time-out. Everyone freeze and chill out for a moment. Imagine the thoughts in a bubble above your head. Imagine the body reactions printed on your torso and the feelings oozing off your shoulders. You will not parent with any effectiveness until you notice and manage those reactions. They are coming between you and your parenting skills—and your child.

Sit down with your partner and go back and review situations where you weren't happy with how they were handled. Fill out the chart below and see what you learn about how you might deal with these more effectively next time. It's a great lesson in awareness and in how you and your partner can support each other and not trigger potentially harmful reactions in each other as you deal with a child you love.

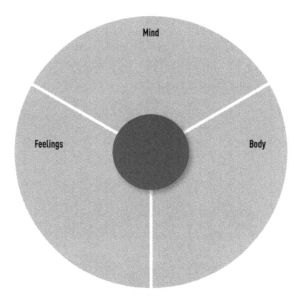

I hope you took the time to at least play out the exercise in your mind. It is only helpful if you personalize it and see how *you* are and how *you* react. It's critical to be specific in any type of training. It isn't enough just to know. You need to play through things in your imagination, the language of the body. The part of you that speaks about it isn't the part that does it. Preparation by pre-playing various scenarios is invaluable.

I haven't even talked about the interaction between the parents. Sometimes one person escalates the reactivity with their observations about what this means and triggers the other parent before the child even comes into it. At other times each parent has a very different view of how serious, dangerous or important the whole issue is. Sometimes one parent sides immediately with the child or commits the child to a certain course of action that can complicate the situation and create other issues between the parents. In extreme situations I have seen parents forgo any parenting rather than go through the unpleasantness of it all, and the child is abandoned. This occurs most often in the teenage years in cases where both parents "give up." Not good for anyone. In the section that follows, I interview Sandra on the building of trust, and we will see how stressful it can be, even when both parents are on the same page and are supporting each other.

Build Trust

This section presents the subject of trust in a realistic light for parents who want to learn more about how to develop trust in their relationships with their children. But rather than get theoretical or hypothetical, I decided it would be more helpful to ask a parent who worked diligently on developing trust with her children to answer a few questions on how she did that—and, since trust is really tested during the hard times, to focus on those times. Sandra has the advantage of being a counselor by training, so she brings a few additional skills to the mix that not everyone possesses.

> *PJ:* How important is it to be consciously working on the development of trust with your child?

> *SS:* It's critical. Children are vulnerable and gullible. They are also astute. I believe **their accomplishments are important, but not as important as their emotional and moral development**. An adult, especially a parent, is the one who looks out for their long-term development. A parent who can't do this can cause a lot of damage. So I always believed that trust was critical for my children's well-being. That meant that whatever I told them had to be the

truth, or a version of the truth that they really needed to know and hear at that time, in a form they could grasp for their age. If at some point in the future they realized that there was another version of the truth, or more complexity to that truth, they also knew I had acted in their best interests at the time. The bottom line here is that **there has to be honesty, and honesty of intention**—and the intention always has to be that it is in their best interests. That is critical.

PJ: Did you ever lose trust?

SS: Not that I'm aware of. I can think of a couple of times when maybe I risked it, perhaps when I was angry and said something that wasn't true and wasn't in their best interests. It may have been about punishment—making them feel hurt or guilty—and not about developing them or improving them. You can get away with that occasionally, because everybody loses it once in a while. Kids know that, just as everybody else does. It becomes a problem when it becomes a pattern and happens more frequently than the focus on development.

PJ: What else did you do to develop trust?

SS: There were several things: showing them I cared and making it obvious by doing things for them, sharing in their happy times, doing things with them that they loved, respecting what was important to them—and making sure they could feel the warmth I felt toward them. Another was being consistently fair, demonstrating that they could trust that I would be fair. It was really about having to question myself, consciously and constantly, about what I was doing and why I was doing it. Even when everybody pretends a decision or action is for the right reasons, if it isn't, the children will know. They may not be able to articulate it or even understand it, and they will often collude with the pretending if you're the parent or the coach—but they will know. I am a firm believer that kids pick up on unconscious intentions. They are willing to be very forgiving of our flaws and weaknesses if our intentions are good. Most children have some kind of ability to screen when your intention is good and when it isn't. So fairness and honesty were very important to me. I wanted the kids to trust me so that they would respect me as a trusted adviser. How else can you be a positive force in their development? If your intentions are truly good for them—and by that I mean they aren't self-serving but are helping them move toward becoming who they need to become, guiding them toward their own highest self—then they will respond better to your influence.

On the other hand, I also believe that people can consciously and dishonestly build trust in children for the purpose of directing and influencing them in ways that are not good for them. I don't think children have particularly good radar for someone who has figured out what children will view as trustworthy behavior and use that to manipulate them. Kids are very vulnerable; they tend to be naturally trusting. But in the end they always figure it out.

PJ: How important was trust when it came to pushing children out of their comfort zones?

SS: Again, it's critical. Certainly I think that in a coaching context the person being coached—whether it's your child, an athlete under your care or someone who reports to you at work—would have to truly trust and believe that you knew better. So even though everything in the child was fighting against what you wanted them to do, at some level the child would have to believe that you knew better. That's trust. The opposite is that the child would feel there was no choice; they were trapped and had to do what you said. That's *not* trust.

Of course, trust goes both ways. Sometimes the parent or the coach trusts that the child will only go so far and then stop. Then, if the child goes beyond that point, trust is affected. There was a time when one of my children lied point-blank to me about missing school. I never thought that would happen. It meant I couldn't trust what that child was telling me. It didn't change how I felt about the child, but it meant I could no longer use what was said as my sole evidence for the questions I needed answered. I knew I needed to have other sources and I had to question more. This child's life changed dramatically for a while.

PJ: Wasn't there a bit of a progression in terms of how much "rope" you gave?

SS: Always. For example, we lived relatively far from many of the kids with whom my son went to school. I often drove him to weekend social events at other people's houses just to help out, to make it easier for him. Often because of the distance he would just stay over. We went through a period, however, when I was worried about what he was into. During that time I made sure I picked him up, no matter what time it was. I just wanted him to know that I would be looking him in the eye that night. He could count on that. He knew why I was picking him up; that had been made clear. He could trust that, rightly or wrongly, there was never going to be the opportunity for me to say, "I didn't know."

I had heard too many stories from parents whose kids got into trouble who said afterward, "I didn't know." They never imagined their child would do what he or she had actually done. For me, it was all about confronting my own naïveté about what my son might find interesting and what he might get into. Now, I was always open and forthright with my son. It wasn't a manipulative kind of thing. It was about stating, "I'm worried about this; therefore, I will be doing this. If you can tell me differently, that this isn't happening, or you want to give me more information, maybe we can negotiate a different plan. But based on the information I have—and here's what it is—this is what we are going to be doing."

PJ: As his mother, you trusted that you knew much better than he did what he needed at the time. Your conviction in staying the course was both admirable and difficult! It was obviously uncomfortable for both of you.

SS: I never felt totally sure I was doing it right. I didn't have a system where I thought, "Okay this is how you do this." I was just doing the best I could to try to get the outcome I knew was best for him. I had confidence that the outcome I wanted was the right one for him in this one particular realm, if not necessarily in his whole development. But I didn't have confidence that I was doing it right.

The question that haunted me, when I say I wasn't sure, was whether this was just teenage experimentation and wasn't going to amount to anything. But he had a friend who I could see was clearly going down the tubes, and my son couldn't see that at all. That was what was scary for me: that he was so blind to the reality of how this other kid's life was going to end up. When I realized he couldn't see it, I had to step in. But because he couldn't see it, he thought I was crazy and overreacting.

In my heart I wondered if I was risking my relationship with him in the long term by being so hard on him. But what's hard on him? Hard on him meant he wasn't happy with me or with his life at home for a while—he was happier with his friends. It's just so difficult to care so much about someone and know they're not happy with you. Nevertheless, the message was always the same, always clear, always honest. I made my intentions explicit, and even though he didn't like what I was doing, he trusted that I believed it was for his good.

There was one time when he wanted to go to a rave. I had allowed him to go to a rave earlier with some friends because it was held at the Science Centre and I thought, "How bad could that be?" But then I did some research on raves and discovered that they had bad press and were clearly connected to drug use. But he begged us to let him go to this particular one—the music was going to be amazing, he said, and some of his friends were going. So I told him, "Okay, maybe I'm misguided here, maybe I need to get more information. I can't believe other parents are letting their children go, but perhaps I need to talk to them and maybe they'll tell me something that will change my mind. Give me the names of some of the parents and I'll call them." He said, "I'm not giving you the names of any parents." I said, "Well then, you're not going."

I remember looking at him and saying, "What parent would let a 15-year-old child go to a drug-laced event in the middle of the night? Who does that? It's not going to be us." I think he could see our logic even though it made him terribly angry. I really did feel bad about it because he desperately wanted to go.

He was a terrific kid, and I felt that if he could see the whole picture he would make better decisions. But how does a 15-year-old grasp the whole picture? I was continually trying to broaden his picture so he could see where we were coming from. But it was almost always a one-way conversation, which made me think he really wasn't listening to a lot of what I had to say, or at least wasn't buying into any of it. I realized, as he got a little older, that he was actually listening very carefully.

I was worried I had damaged my relationship with him because maybe I had been impugning him unfairly. I asked him, a couple of years later, "Was I too hard on you?" and he said, "No, Mom, you weren't." That was good enough for me. He is now 26 and we thoroughly enjoy each other's company. We have a very respectful and loving relationship.

PJ: Now with your stepdaughter, who came to you when she was 14, it was very different, wasn't it? She was starting into a new school late in the year, a few weeks after the beginning of a semester.

SS: Our relationship was a little purer, less contaminated by history. I had a much more objective perspective on what she needed and what was good for her. She was behind in school and feeling fragile because of that, and there was so much work to do, but she had a lot to gain from proving she was capable. It helped, too, that she was not interested in anything remotely related to the usual teenage propensity to experiment with trouble. She was a willing partner in her own growth and development. A large part of building trust with her was about honesty around what would be best for her. I had a lot of faith that she was a regular kid who just needed the right environment for her personality, and that given the chance to do her own thing and be appreciated, she would blossom. I had total confidence in her abilities and that's probably why she trusted me, because she knew that. She knew I believed she was capable.

She trusted that both you and I would be fair and would see the good things in her. Children use the faces of their parents like a mirror reflecting back to them how lovable they are. That's where their self-image comes from.

She could trust that when she looked at us she would see herself in a positive light—in an optimistic, hopeful, expectant-that-she-could-do-things-right light. That is a very big element of trust, and it's another way of talking about it. If you are my parent, and I can see the best I can be coming back at me when you look at me, that is a very powerful force. There is a respect for what is in me, and an expectation that I will rise to it.

PJ: But that has to be backed up by experience. The child needs some successes to reinforce that image and therefore you, as a parent, need to have some sense of progression in terms of what they are capable of at any given moment.

SS: I had to be very careful in the beginning, and yet there was a lot to be done. I had to provide support and ensure that she had some success. I also had to be careful that there was no colluding with the part of her that believed she was incapable and incompetent and all that kind of stuff. There was no "Oh, she can't do this, I'd better fix it," or "I'd better let her off the hook," or "I should go in and talk to them at the school, she can't do this, this isn't fair, this isn't right."

There were some rough nights as she worked to catch up, and the school didn't cut her a lot of slack, I must say. The plan, in terms of progression, was that we would tackle one project at a time, and nothing else would matter right then. And when the next thing came up we would tackle that.

It's the old "I will lend to you my belief in you until you develop your own." That belief in herself came slowly but steadily. With it rose her sense of herself as capable and lovable. So the progression was "Let's just get you steady on your feet first. Let's get you to see that you are just as smart and just as capable as everybody else, and then maybe we'll start to move to the harder stuff." But she was truly like a flower opening. We just had to provide the right environment for her and the right kind of support.

PJ: But sometimes it's also recognizing that you may not be the one to take someone all the way, in every area of their development. In this case, you had some allies. You used an educational consultant and you found a school that fit her. At one point she had a bit of tutoring in writing skills. The timing of those things was important.

SS: That's about *being attuned to what this person needs each step along the way.* I was very attuned to what she needed, but I didn't know how to find all of it myself. I didn't know how to find a school for her, for example, but I knew what she needed. The consultant asked me a few key questions about her and then said, "Okay, here's the kind of school I think she needs. Go talk to the principal of this school and see what you think." The principal's whole philosophy for her was "Of course you can do this, absolutely you can do this—and by the way, if on occasion you decide *not* to do it, we will be phoning your parents and telling them about it, because there is absolutely no reason for you not to be able to do it." That was the message we all needed to hear at that point.

In both instances, with my son and stepdaughter, it was the same: they both had boundaries they couldn't go outside of but within which they had lots of room to move. They also knew that I, and everyone else around them who mattered, was saying, "I know what you are capable of and I will not let you escape that. You can make your bed poorly in the morning; you can get angry; you can lament your life's hardships—but there are certain things you will be held accountable for: rising to meet your own potential, and finding out who you are when you are at your best and feel most alive."

PJ: But there was also a consistent message being reinforced. The principal, for example, was giving your stepdaughter the same message you were giving—and that wasn't an accident. Whether it was from her figure-skating coach, her teachers, her tutor, or you, or me, her father, we were all giving her the same "can do" message. But what happens when an outsider, like a school principal, teacher or sport coach, is on a different wavelength than the parent?

SS: It's absolutely imperative that everyone works together, because in the case of the school principal, for example, if I am a "difficult" parent and the principal is trying hard to develop this child, he's a doomed man. He has picked up on what the child needs, but I as a parent am not "getting it." Or worse, I'm undermining it or sabotaging it. The child may still perform well academically, but she might also get weaker emotionally. It's like when an athlete has a "crazy" mother or father but a good coach. The coach is working hard to build some normalcy, feeding back to the child how well they are doing or where they are going to have to bear down, but the parent is undermining that or weakening the child by indulging them or criticizing them.

The reverse is also true. You can have a technically superior coach who is poorly intentioned in terms of overall development but is saying all the right words. The parent trusts the coach instead of looking out for their child's long-term development; the child appears to be successful, so they abdicate to the coach. But the coach isn't looking out for the emotional and moral growth of the child, just the physical success. The parents trust that coach without really looking into their behavior or ethics. They have blind trust. And if the parents trust the coach, then usually the child will believe that the coach must be right even if this "doesn't feel right." This can lead to many types of problems—including abuse.

We have a friend whose son played for a coach who treated his own son, who was one of the team's best players, very badly. She and her husband had a good social relationship with the coach and his wife at the time, but she was concerned about his treatment of his son, and asked me what I thought. In a nutshell, my thoughts were: It isn't good for your son to be seeing all the adults in his life colluding with the coach's behavior. His behavior toward his son is wrong, it is bad for his son, and nobody is saying anything about it. At some level your son knows this is not good for this boy, and he sees all these adults, including his own parents, observing it but not saying anything about it. Children learn from watching. They are expert observers.

This is another place where trust comes in. Do the parents "walk the walk"? How can you say he is a good coach when you can see that what he is doing in this situation is so damaging? I think her son, who is now 16, has explicit trust in his parents because they have acted with integrity in every situation (and competitive hockey provides many), including this one. They changed teams even though the team was highly successful and it caused a lot of trouble to do so.

I think that "walk the walk" behavior is more important than anything. Consistency and honesty, even when it isn't convenient—especially when it isn't convenient—build trust big time. You don't just mouth empty words when a situation comes up; you act. Now, you may make a mistake, you can miss the cues, you may be afraid to act, but if you are up-front about it and admit you made a mistake, you can recover and regain trust because the child then thinks, "Okay, what I thought was a betrayal of our values, of what we believe in, was just that. You made a mistake in judgment here." It's not that one has to be perfect all the time. But you do have to be conscious that everything you are saying and doing sends a message, and every time you are silent when you shouldn't be, it tells a story. That was actually one of my biggest fears: that I would be silent when I shouldn't be and that I would speak when I shouldn't. That's the part I never felt sure of, but I decided to err on the side of speaking up rather than being silent.

PJ: You need to have a good backbone to do any of this stuff. You need to have a good backbone any time you are developing another person.

SS: It's very tiring. It can also be scary, and sometimes it's hurtful. There were nights when I felt really hurt by certain reactions from the kids. I remember writing letters that I never gave them about how angry and upset I was. I am sure coaches feel like that when they have knocked themselves out for a kid and then the kid does something stupid.

PJ: Any closing comments?

SS: It is totally worth it. It is a true test of oneself. I have never found anything in life that tested me emotionally and morally the way raising children did. One has to be rigorously honest with oneself. That is one of the things I like most about having a developmental bias when working with someone. You have to grow yourself. You can't slack off, you can't make excuses. It's a great challenge. And rewarding. It isn't easy, but it's a lot of fun. We had a lot of fun.

Encourage and Use Imagery

It's important that you paint clear pictures of what you want for children. "Don't make a mess, the house was just cleaned" is not as visual as giving them some specifics about how you want their room to look. But what I really want to talk about here is *keeping the skill of imagery alive in your children.* Very young children have vivid imagery skills and, indeed, rarely distinguish between the imaginary world and the real world. Picture a child running through a room of adults with arms outstretched in wing position buzzzzzzzzzing loudly like an airplane! Sadly, this often gets stamped out of them in school.

I pulled the following quote from Sandra's teaching notes for her work with young figure skaters: "Any movement requires an accompanying image, whether we are conscious of it or not. It is your nervous system, not your musculature, that determines the pattern, sequence and timing of your movements. When you imagine an activity, as far as your nervous system is concerned you are doing it."

This has serious implications for children in sport, dance or any activity involving movement. Many research studies have shown that mentally practicing a motor skill can be as valuable as actually practicing the skill physically. There are times where it is not possible to practice—but you can do it in your mind, using as many of the senses as possible. It's important to make it as real as possible.

This quote from Sandra's talk to older skaters is also good advice for teenagers or for those needing to impress others, whether it's in an interview or interacting with their teachers. It's about being conscious of the image of yourself and your capabilities that you project to others:

> "As you take responsibility for your own thoughts, you must watch how you describe yourself to others. When sharing a problem you should also share what you are doing to solve that problem. That is the image people will carry around with them, giving you added support for the change."

When I am working with athletes who need to impress upon the head coach that they are getting better, I always have them talk to the coach about the changes they are trying to make and to paint a picture of how they are going about it. Since the coach is the one who will decide who makes the Olympic team, and who plays and who doesn't, this is important, because it creates a clear image for him or her of what the athlete is doing and how this is a positive step. It also makes the coach more inclined to cut the athlete some breathing space while they are trying to make the change.

Children who are a bit older, teenagers, need to know that using imagery is a way for them to take an active role in getting what they want. They also need to understand that this isn't just dreaming. There is a major difference between imagery and fantasy. They both use inner images about things that would be wonderful to have in our lives, but imagery develops our potential, whereas fantasy causes it to stagnate. The biggest difference really has to do with the intention we bring to them. When we use imagery, we make a commitment to move toward what we want and we develop the belief that it's possible. Fantasies, however, set impossible goals, rely on luck or good fortune for their realization, and absorb energy that might better be expended in moving toward what we can *really* accomplish.

Young performers need to understand the discipline and intention in using imagery to improve their performance, self-esteem, or whatever they are working on. Most people are fairly adept at the visual thinking we do every day as we plan and organize our daily activities. However, **it takes conscious effort on the part of the performer to move to more sophisticated and powerful mental images** that need to be practiced daily if performance is to improve. In most imagery concerning physical skills, the kinesthetic sense—an awareness of the position and movement of the body's voluntary muscles—is particularly important.

Ask your children what they are imagining and how they see themselves. It can be very revealing. Quite a few years ago, in the late afternoon of New Year's Eve in 1992, Sandra and I gave each of our four children, then ranging in age from 8 to 16, a set of crayons/markers/pens and asked them to imagine and capture on a flip-chart page their life on New Year's Eve 2000. What sorts of things might they be engaged in eight years hence? Sandra and I also did the exercise. Later, at dinner, each person in turn showed the others what they had drawn and written on their page, and explained it. We still have those sheets, but I don't even need to look at them to remember; for example, my daughter Carlye, who was then 14, talking about going to medical school and traveling. It's interesting to look back on that time now that she is practicing medicine, having spent a year in India between her undergraduate years and medical school. This exercise was really a lot of fun. The kids enjoyed it once they got into it, and Sandra and I got insight into their hopes and aspirations, and what they were imagining.

Now, this wasn't something we held them to. It was just an exercise that we all enjoyed. It is not to be confused with the goal-setting we used when we had things we wanted to see happen. In those instances we really helped them focus on the performance goal—their next step—and not the end goal. As was pointed out in the main section of this book, the end goal can often feel overwhelming. Sandra's comment on our daughter's homework in the trust section is a good example of this.

Patience is also critical for both parent and child. You can instill patience by breaking things up into small, doable steps that allow children to see real progress. Relief—and increased confidence—comes with the completion of each step, not just at the end of a very long process.

For children whose vivid imaginations often lead to nightmares, there needs to be careful monitoring of their imagery "diet." Images will stay with them for a long time and seem real, creating real fear in them. The image may be in the imagination, but the fear is in the body and is real. It is important not to minimize their experience and to respect the power the image has over the child—not to be in awe of it, but find a way to talk about it.

When Dane, our son, was very young, he had a recurring dream of being chased by a wolf. He would wake up and call out anxiously. One night Sandra went in and sat on his bed to work with the image. She had him imagine the wolf chasing him, then had him stop and face the wolf and ask him what he wanted, why he was chasing Dane. The wolf, in Dane's imagination, said he wanted to play. "Oh," Sandra said, "*that's* why he's chasing you, he wants to play with you!"

Buoyed by this experience, I went into his bedroom one evening when he was having another nightmare. I asked him about it and then suggested that he "change the channel" on his "TV." I asked him where he had fun and enjoyed being, and his immediate response was "At the cottage with all the kids." I suggested he change channels and watch that instead. I got back in bed and Sandra asked me how I'd managed to get him quiet so quickly. I proudly informed her that we sport-psych people had a few skills for such moments. We were just nicely falling asleep when Dane called out, "Dad, I don't get that channel!"

Uncover and Work Through Blocks

Basketball coach Sam Mitchell comments that the hardest thing for many people, in any endeavor, is to step out of their comfort zone. And that's precisely what you will be asking people to do, on occasion, when you take on the developmental mandate. This will be especially challenging for them when they feel blocked; when they think they aren't making any progress and it's clear that what they need to do is to try something new or different. I like the yardstick Sam uses at these times. He points out that with young performers, there will be ups and downs that you can live with if the consistency of effort is there. In other words, if you see the effort but not the results, that's okay for a while. Just reward their effort as they try to get better and overcome whatever's blocking them from breaking through to the next level.

For parents, the first step is to find out—get clarity—on what the block is. Is it a lack of confidence? Is it a lack of competence? How do the children see it? Do they have clarity or is it more like a fog of uncertainty?

Asking questions is the only means of uncovering what is really in the way. Think back to the story of the swimmer in Chapter 6 who had stopped trying and who believed, down deep, that the block probably meant she didn't have the talent because swimming faster was becoming harder and harder. If we were her parents, and took as our only reference point her external behavior and constantly reacted to that, then we would believe that she was lazy or not willing to push herself. Our comments, focused on those beliefs, would be way off base, and far from dealing with the real issue, would probably succeed only in damaging our relationship with her.

Of course this also applies to any block in any area of a child's development. Sometimes children have a block they struggle with in a subject at school. My daughter Erika had a block when it came to writing and expressing her thoughts in an organized, coherent manner. It took only four sessions with an experienced former teacher for Erika not only to overcome her block but to begin to flourish and take great pride in her writing skills. It was really quite astounding how quickly she progressed once the real block was uncovered and dealt with. A few focused questions, a new way of looking at the challenge, and boom—a totally different outcome.

There is no value in having a solution to the wrong problem, and you can only discover the true nature of what's in the way if you dig. If you remember what was discussed in the Blocks chapter earlier in the book, you already know that when you ask good questions, your children will actually end up doing the digging themselves!

It's also important that you don't get caught up in other people's ideas of what is "right." So, after discovering what's standing in your child's way, put on your creative-thinking hat and help them come up with a personalized way for dealing with the block.

As with many things, planning will go a long way in alleviating blocks or making it easier to deal with them. A good method is to have a pre-school-year meeting with your kids to discuss commitments and expectations related to school and extracurricular activities. My children were given the option of certain activities—piano lessons, guitar lessons, hockey, figure skating—but each child needed to understand up front the commitment they were making. Once they chose something, they were committed to it until the season ended, at which point they could drop out if they wished. This saved a lot of headaches and sometimes led to some interesting sequels at the end of summer, when suddenly the child went back into something he or she had voiced displeasure about during the preceding year!

Embrace Adversity

I recently attended the wedding of an athlete who had been a very good point guard in university basketball. Sara's coach, Stu, was the emcee at her wedding, and when we were talking at the reception, he told me something interesting. Every year, even with university-aged students, he was getting more and more phone calls from parents unhappy that their daughter was going through some adversity relating to basketball. She might have been pulled from a game early for poor effort on defense, or she wasn't a starter because she was struggling with her shooting.

Stu's point was that the parents were trying to spare their children any adversity. As a developer of people, that worried him, because often it is by facing and dealing with adversity that we "get the message" and move to the next level in our play. Even more important, it's when we move to the next level as a person. He wondered, as an aside, if this was in any way connected to the increased number of suicides each year on campus. Are we raising children incapable of dealing with real life by trying to shield them from adverse experiences?

I was thinking about this as I read an article claiming that children in some Western cultures live in an environment that is too clean. The article asserted that compared with those of us who grew up in less sanitized times, kids today "don't eat enough dirt" when they are young and therefore haven't built up the defense system needed to combat germs.

This is an area, dealing with adversity, where we can have a profound and lasting developmental impact on our children. They are often much more open to parenting/coaching when they are in a pickle. How we handle these situations that they perceive as almost life-threatening (at least in the teenage years) can solidify our long-term relationship with our children. But be prepared for the reality that later, they won't likely acknowledge or even remember the incident, let alone the fact that you were instrumental in assisting them in dealing with it.

Our four children, as I write this, range in age from 26 to 34, with kids of their own, and Sandra, in particular, is a sought-after resource for them on many matters. This is a direct result of her assistance in dealing with numerous circumstances of extreme adversity—or at least that's how our kids viewed them at the time. Today, when we talk about any adversity that occurred when they were in high school, it is dramatically downplayed, as in "It wasn't that bad, and I had a handle on it." That's when you know you did a decent job—when they feel they really didn't need, or get, much help.

It is not my intention here to repeat what has been discussed elsewhere in this book, but I do want to remind you that the reframing information is of real value when dealing with adversity. The Manage Yourself chapter is another good one to review—if you can stay cool through the adversity, you will have done a fine job as a parent.

Here is one more thing I have found invaluable in my work with young athletes and my own children. Help your children differentiate between *what* they are doing and *who* they are; between where the activity ends and where they begin. Let me explain.

They can be terribly upset with something that happened, such as the result of a game, how they played that game or what they did at a particular moment, and yet be okay with themselves. *They* are not the last conversation they had with a friend, or the final score, or the argument. They are separate from that. When they become what they are doing, they pay too big a price when they fail. On top of the setback, their self-esteem takes a huge whack. I caution athletes not to overpay for a setback by giving away the very thing they most need to recover from it: confidence.

This chapter on parenting is meant to be supplementary to, not separate from, the rest of the book, which contains plenty of information that is applicable to the parenting role. So if you find a section here inadequate in depth, put on your parental specs and go back and reread the main work. You'll find lots more there that you can apply in your most important job!

Parents who extinguish the Third Factor in their children tend to:
- Replicate their dysfunctional upbringing with their offspring.
- Lack awareness of how they interact and therefore are often much too prone to react.
- Abandon or micromanage in times of crisis or adversity.

Parents who ignite the Third Factor in their children:
- Are aware and therefore often wonder whether they are doing the right thing. As a result they seek out information on their role from other sources. They ignite their own Third Factor so they can ignite their child's.
- Communicate effectively and on a consistent basis with their children. Instead of giving in to the impulse to react, they ask questions, listen, communicate clear expectations, and make sure the child understands not only the "what" but also the "why."
- Are often more empathetic than sympathetic. Empathy is more developmental.

Editor: That was certainly worth pushing for. It will be greatly appreciated by our readers.

Author: We really could have written another book on the topic.

Editor: True. But with the first seven chapters as a lead-in, it's as complete as it needs to be.

Author: So we have really written a parenting book disguised as a business book?

Editor: Let's not get silly at the end here, or people will think we don't get along. This was a fun project. What are you going to write next?

Author: Children's books.

Editor: I'm serious.

Author: So am I.

Editor: What's the first one called then?

Author: The Belly Button Monster.

Editor: The Belly Button Monster? What's it about?

Author: You'll just have to wait and see . . .

Conclusion

So you've decided to be an Igniter, a leader who enables others to excel at whatever it is they are doing. As you've discovered in reading this book, to do so you will need a strong developmental bias—the intrinsic need to grow and develop people. You develop this bias and become an Igniter by doing the following: managing yourself; building trust; using your imagination and imagery and encouraging others to do the same; uncovering and working through blocks; and embracing adversity when it arises. All of this is in service of getting the people in your care—whether they're employees, athletes or offspring—excited about and engaged in being the best they can be and committed to themselves and their own development. Committed, in other words, to igniting their own Third Factor.

At the end of every interview with each of the six coaches featured in this book, I asked them, "If you had only two minutes to convey what you have learned about developing others—igniting the Third Factor in other people—what would you say?" Their answers differed only in the words they chose. They were unanimous on the point of the coach's need to focus on the person being developed, and to engage with that person. Here are a few of their comments:

Mel Davidson: "The people you are working with will be tomorrow's leaders and tomorrow's society, so whatever you do with them . . . that is what society is going to look like tomorrow. That's a huge responsibility, and how you act and how you talk to them and whether you respect them or disrespect them—whatever you do—that's what things are going to look like."

Frank Dick: "I went to a wedding in San Diego years ago. Out of the blue the bride hit me between the eyes with a piece of wisdom. She said, 'Frankie I wish you the strength to give your children the only two gifts you can and must give them as a parent: the roots to grow and the wings to fly.' In a stroke she summed up the whole business of coaching and developing people."

David Hemery: "Trust that your athletes can provide you with even more information than you can see. Ask them first what their experience was before you come in with your feedback. Always start with them so you are generating their awareness, their responsibility, their ownership—you are valuing them and their experience."

Andy Higgins: "Understand that it's all about the human experience, what happens to a human being . . . the most important thing that is happening here is with and for the other person and your opportunities to personally learn from that."

Debbie Muir: "Your job as coach is to connect athletes to higher performance. In order to do that, you need to be aware of yourself and all the things you do, and how that gets translated into your day-to-day practice with your athletes. So on the one side it's all about the athlete—not the coach—and on the other side it's all about the coach."

Gary Winckler: "You always want to develop the person. It's the coach's responsibility to help this person become more responsible, so there are times when you have to be able to shift responsibility to them. There has to be a leader in the process."

We have covered much ground since I introduced you to the concept of the Third Factor. The quotes above from the six "Igniters" interviewed all emphasize the need to engage with the other person, something you can't possibly do by staying in your office and working on "getting things done." You need to be out there where it's happening, on the "playing field." You need to be listening, observing, providing guidance—not in an intrusive, micromanaging way but in a developmental way.

At the end of the day your reputation as a leader will be determined by what those you have managed have to say about you and about the time spent under your care. If in 20 years someone now in a leadership role still remembers and speaks of you as an amazing manager whose inspired guidance directly influenced them and contributed to their present success, then you will have done your job as an Igniter. You will have left a legacy. Because the highest praise you can ever receive from another person is the acknowledgment "I am where I am today because of you; I couldn't have done it without you."

Best of luck in your igniting endeavors!

Be a "Positive Participant" in Your Child's Athletics

By Sandra Stark

Sport needs good leadership, particularly sport for children. It always has and it always will. Harry Edwards, a well-known sport sociologist, showed us clearly that sport is value neutral. It is neither good nor bad: it takes on the values of the people in charge and the culture in which it is housed. You need only look at sport in the United States versus Canada versus the former USSR to see different values expressed and reinforced.

Jim Coleman, another sport sociologist, spent his life looking at the role sport plays in a culture. He showed that there is no proof that kids who are involved in sport do better in life than kids who hang around in malls. To many, this seems counterintuitive. Certainly most parents believe that kids are better off in sport. They believe that sport has the potential to build character—or they wouldn't enroll their children. The fact is, sport can be a source of positive growth and development in a child, or sport can do great damage. Unless it is in the hands of someone who is focused on growth and development, you won't get growth and development. It doesn't just occur naturally because it is baseball. It depends on the values of the people, the league and the culture.

The Importance of the Parent

Many parents today know this. They couldn't tell you about Harry Edwards or Jim Coleman, but they spend time learning the values of the coach or supervisor to whom they are handing over their child. If those values aren't clear, or a parent mistrusts them, they will keep a very close watch. What can be more difficult for parents is to turn the same questioning eye inward and ensure that they remain a positive participant in the culture of sport—that they too are working to contribute to their child's growth and development through sport.

My interest in this topic comes out of being a parent and working with so many athletes and parents over the years—and watching parents struggle to stay grounded in the competitive arena. Originally, I assumed that this struggle was largely a result of the very high levels of competition I was working at—mostly at the Olympic level, where the pressure to succeed is intense. Recently, though, more and more people have come to me with an increasing number of problems with parents at a much lower level of competition. So how come? Is there something inherent in sport at all levels that makes it difficult for parents?

To discover the answer to this question, I only had to go back to my experience as a parent to remember how difficult it was emotionally to stay centered. A quote by Elizabeth Stone sums up the source of this difficulty perfectly: "Making the decision to have a child—it's momentous. It is to decide forever to have your heart go walking outside your body."

Be a Positive Participant

If you have read this far, I will assume that you have a child and that they are probably involved, or considering becoming involved, in sport in some way. What follows are four guidelines to keep in mind as you help your child navigate the peaks and valleys that accompany participating in any sport. These are ways in which you can help make sport a positive experience for your child. They came about as a result of a phone-in show on this topic that I conducted on CBC Radio and a subsequent speech delivered to coaches from across Ontario. They represent my thoughts and lessons learned over years of experience.

Four (Not So) Easy Tips on Being a Positive Participant

Provide continuous positive reinforcement. Positive reinforcement is the single most important factor in performance. Remember that reinforcing effort is far more beneficial than reinforcing success (e.g., "You were really working hard out there! You never gave up!").

Focus on confidence. You need to always be working on building confidence. This doesn't necessarily mean praise; it means that there is no question in your child's mind that your love and acceptance of them is not tied to their performance on the field in any way.

If it has been a bad game, point out something that the child can do something about. It is important to attribute the problem to something within the child's control (e.g., "You just need to get near the ball more often—but hey, you touched it five times this week, as opposed to only twice last week!")

Fear ("You're going to get dropped from the team!") and rejection ("Don't speak to me right now") may get results temporarily, but neither is good over the long haul because they impact your child's confidence at a very deep level. Attempting to motivate in this way will carve a big hole of fear and self-contempt in your child, and ultimately damage your relationship.

John Wooden, the legendary NCAA basketball coach, used the following feedback mix: 75 percent specific instruction, 12 percent requests to hustle, 7 percent praise, 6 percent scolds. This applies to coaching of course. Obviously working to such specifics as a parent is impossible because you are not teaching the skills yourself, but the general idea holds: negative feedback does not lead to great successes. You are the parent for life, not for a three-year contract as some of these seemingly successful "negative" coaches are.

Work on your emotional discipline. Athletes need to continuously learn, re-learn, and improve their emotional discipline as they work to improve their skills under increasing levels of pressure. You are your child's first and most important teacher. If you can't control yourself on the sidelines, it is unreasonable to expect your child to do so on the actual field.

It is extremely difficult to watch your child out there, but you need to recognize that you must learn along with your child. Learn to recognize your own habits and limitations. If staying in control is something you struggle with, prepare ahead of time.

Be a parent, not another coach. As a parent, you must look at the bigger picture—not just help your child become a better hockey or soccer player. Your job is to make sure that they are becoming stronger and better as a person.

Kids can be very vulnerable to thinking they are no good, that they are failures. If they are to build character, they need a parent to help them make sense of some of the disappointments and setbacks, and show them how to handle the successes.

Some of the decisions the coach has to make are hard on kids. Parents need to help them frame them, understand them, gain back their perspective, and point out how well they are doing. Most important, as mentioned above, your child should never feel that your love and acceptance is in any way tied to athletic performance.

If you consciously work on the four areas above, your child's experience with sport will be a tremendously positive one—and that's something we can all cheer about.

APPENDIX B

When All Else Fails

This section is different from the rest in that it is instructional in nature. It is a summary of a two-day program called Tackling Challenging Conversations that we offer through our company, Performance Coaching. There is an awful lot of information here, so take your time in reading it.

onfrontation occurs when we encounter resistance to a change we want a valued performer to make. But before we can even begin to look at the "how to" of having these sometimes difficult conversations, we need to confront our own reluctance or inability to do so.

What is your habitual reaction to situations of potential conflict? I can tell you mine—I run! I have avoided conflict ever since I can remember—until a few years ago, when I finally learned how to confront.

We all have our own beliefs, images and preconceived ideas of what conflict is about. These beliefs have grown out of our history with conflict, as well as how it was handled in our families or by our significant teachers, and in our culture. Our own personalities, and the beliefs and responses we have developed to accommodate our temperament, will have also determined our relationship to conflict.

But it is painfully clear even to those of us who hate confronting that we cannot make people better if we are unwilling or unable to have that difficult conversation when it is needed. Awkward or unpleasant though it might be for us, we have to do it. If we don't, we'll leave people floundering and we won't be igniting anything—least of all the Third Factor.

The concept of confrontation, and the effect it can have on growth and development, could really fit into any of the five areas we've discussed in this book. For it to be an effective tool it requires excellent self-management skills; if it is done effectively it builds trust; it is often vital in the recognition and removal of blocks and the ability to embrace adversity.

Most of us find confrontational conversations difficult, and we don't look forward to them in the least. But what follows is an effort to provide you with a map you can refer to—to help you feel more confident and comfortable—going into these difficult conversations. The map is merely a representation of the territory—but it's a big help when you're lost or need direction.

An important thing to keep in mind is that no one expects you to be perfect. **If the other person knows that you care and have their best interests at heart, they will be forgiving** when you aren't fully present or aren't doing things exactly as you "ought" to. They'll cut you some slack if, on occasion, you haven't provided perfect feedback. Your good intentions are like money in the bank for days when you aren't as sharp as you ought to be.

Challenging Conversations: What Are They?

In a working environment there are generally three kinds of challenging conversations. All of them require a change in behavior, though the reasons for this differ.

The first is performance related: you need someone to change how they are performing a certain task. They may not be aware that change is necessary, they may not believe it's necessary, or they may not want to make the change. But in your opinion, things do have to change.

In the second case, a difficult personality is wreaking havoc on relationships, office morale, team development and/or productivity.

In the third case, it isn't that the person is doing something wrong or poorly, but the hard truth—which has to be faced—is that the effort isn't working for the overall good of the team or company. If your marketing plan isn't getting results, if the corporate culture is having a detrimental effect on your people, if people aren't working well together as a team, then there's going to have to be a discussion to identify problems and negotiate solutions. They are going to have to face certain facts or realities that they have been avoiding or missing.

The Four Steps

Here are the four steps we focus on in our Tackling Challenging Conversations program.

- **Step One: Analyze** the situation, and **prepare** yourself for the conversation.
- **Step Two:** Prepare and deliver an **opening statement**.
- **Step Three: Explore reality** through discussion to develop a full understanding of the problem.
- **Step Four:** Create a **plan to resolve** the problem.

Before we head into these steps, let's take a broader look at the challenge of having difficult conversations so you can begin to see the need for all the upfront work that will ensure your effectiveness in a confrontation.

What Makes This So Difficult?

In the period prior to a confrontation there is a lead-up time where we are gathering data, courage and, often, steam! In this anticipatory stage it's easy to start creating scary scenarios in your imagination of what *could* happen. You boil up an emotional soup of blame, indignation and anger. Your creative energy is being channeled into seemingly righteous anger that may make you feel powerful but can actually be quite debilitating, undermining your ability to do a good job. It is therefore crucial that you learn to manage the additional pressure you're feeling about a confrontation before it occurs, and to concentrate on the interpersonal and communication skills that you normally carry out well.

What Are You Afraid Of?

What makes these conversations so difficult before you even start them? What scares you and causes the increased pressure? Managers in our courses come up with lengthy lists, which include fear of making the situation worse, escalating the problem; fear of being rejected, losing the relationship, suffering retaliation; fear of being met with irrationality or emotional outbursts; fear of hurt feelings.

So, you may be thinking, given how much trouble this is, why bother? What if I just let it go and do nothing? Here are a few of the thoughts from the same workshop group on why *not* confronting is a bad idea: the problem escalates rather than being resolved, emotions build until someone blows up, I lose the relationship, I lose my credibility with other staff, I undermine my health and myself, I could lose my job.

If I confront, I'm worried about getting an outcome I don't want. If I don't confront, I'm practically guaranteed of getting an outcome I don't want—the only difference is that the timing is slower and less predictable!

In the face of this apparently balanced scale of pros and cons, some of us continue to feel that it is safer not to confront. But why do you think that is? It's because **in your mind you are holding this conversation as a threat.** You are experiencing it through your internal imagery and talking to yourself about it as if it is a threat. It's this perception that causes a lot of problems. Most people will delay having to deal with something they feel is a threat. The result, however, is that in the delayed time period, feelings of frustration and anger build as infractions continue and compound, while the offender remains oblivious.

If you believe a conversation to resolve an issue is a threat and are preparing for it as if it were a threat, what is the most likely thing to occur internally? Fear. Anger. The creation of a self-fulfilling prophecy. You confront from a place of fear or anger (blame, punishment, guilt, intimidation, embarrassment), which is a place of reaction, defensiveness and irrationality. Fear and anger are not good internal states from which to confront. They undermine your skills and reduce your choices for how to conduct yourself.

You need to have tremendous clarity up front if you want to confront in an effective way and from a position of higher purpose. So what are the opportunities in confronting?

You want the people you coach to trust you, but many people mistakenly equate trust in a relationship with lack of discord. They couldn't be more wrong. An ability to deal with discord and learn how to navigate through it is one of the biggest determinants of how much trust people have in one another. Discord, disagreement, and difficult topics are absolutely unavoidable in authentic relationships and always present an opportunity to deepen the trust—or weaken it.

In Chapter 3, Manage Yourself, we saw how certain beliefs can limit your effectiveness as a coach. For example, if you tell yourself that people will trust you if you're nice to them and easy to get along with, you're deluding yourself. This is not what builds trust. You will never confront effectively as long as you hold this faulty belief.

Sometimes you might be afraid that if you bring a problem to someone's attention, they won't trust you anymore—they'll feel betrayed, hurt, criticized. This too is not true. If you are coaching me, my trust in you is built on the knowledge that you will act responsibly, honorably and fairly in helping me improve, not that you will chicken out and leave me hanging by not telling me when I'm doing something wrong, making a bad impression or messing up.

To engage in this process successfully, you have to be big. And that's hard, really hard, when you're angry, frustrated, rushed or embarrassed, or your neck is on the line and you know you're right but someone is resisting. I think intuitively we all know this and at some level fear we just can't be that big, or think we shouldn't have to be ("He shouldn't have put me in that position"), or just plain don't want to be.

So we would rather not risk making matters worse—at least that's how we talk about it. It comes out in phrases such as "I'll just make matters worse," "It won't make any difference," "It won't be a positive experience in the end," or "People may get hurt, or angry, behave badly, or relations will suffer." We rarely say: "I'm just not a big enough person to pull this off" or "I don't know how to do this."

Your purpose as a leader is to help someone get better at whatever it is they have to do, even if it requires you to confront them. The question is not whether to confront or not; it is how do you confront in a way that communicates your best intentions and meets your highest purpose. How do you confront with confidence that you will do no harm—to the other person or yourself?

Achieving Clarity for Yourself

All of us could use some helpful coaching in these situations, but one needs to be able to coach oneself as well. In the imagery section we made it clear that until you can imagine your path, your actions and the desired outcome, it is difficult, if not impossible, to accomplish tasks effectively. This is especially true of confronting.

The first point of intervention for a coach/leader, therefore, is clarity. Let's look at how important clarity is in confronting someone by examining the role of clarity in each of the four confronting steps we identified above:

- **Step One: Analyze and Prepare:** I need to have tremendous clarity myself about the intention of this conversation, how I want to act and the gap I want closed.

- **Step Two: Prepare and Deliver an Opening Statement:** I need to provide clarity to my partner, and be able and willing to communicate my perspective and the problem we must solve together. I should therefore prepare and practice my opening statement.

- **Step Three: Explore Reality:** I need to have clarity on the other person's perspective, reaction, and needs; I need to understand how they view the situation.

- **Step Four: Resolve and Plan:** I need to have clarity about how to move forward; to use the mutual respect and clearer understanding of each other's point of view that this process has illuminated to decide how we can proceed together.

Moving forward *together* is of utmost importance. It's key to your ability to coach someone, because you can't do that with any hope of success without the other person's confidence, trust and respect. This entire model is designed to build trust and respect while confronting someone with difficult information. We will progress through the model, continuing to move back and forth between *what you need to do in the conversation* and *what you need to do in yourself.*

Step One: Analyze and Prepare

Step One is something you do on your own. It's about preparing yourself for the confrontation by analyzing the situation and trying to form a clear picture of how it might be resolved. It's about taking the time to gain clarity and insight.

The three key questions in this stage are:

1. What is the overarching purpose of this conversation?
2. How do I want to present myself (behave)?
3. What, specifically, is the problem (the gap I want closed)?

1. What is the overarching purpose of this conversation?

Being clear about the purpose is perhaps the most important consideration when you're about to confront someone. It is absolutely critical that
you hold that purpose front and center in your preparation and execu-
tion. It is how you will measure and evaluate your own performance in
the ensuing interaction. The crucial question will be "Did this conversation fulfill its purpose?"

Clarify your intent in your own mind. Nail it down. Too many things
can come at you during the interaction that could knock you off balance
or distract you from your purpose if you don't have it clearly articulated
in your mind.

Your ability to manage yourself well hinges on what you believe to
be your overall purpose in having this conversation. This is the biggest
test of the skills we cover in Chapter 3. First, you have to know what you
ultimately want for this person and for yourself. You have to look past
the conversation and how you are feeling, and focus on your developmental bias.

If, upon self-examination, you discover that what you want to achieve
is more about blaming, punishing or humiliating than it is about developing this person, then you need to admit to yourself that this is not a
good purpose and hold off having the conversation until you've brought
your feelings into line. You need to consider that maybe you're not ready,
or that a different conversation is needed. If, on the other hand, you're
convinced that the impending confrontation is what the person needs if
they're going to move forward, then you can feel confident about it even
if you're nervous. But you still have to make sure that the words you
choose communicate your good intention, and that some of your other
feelings (perhaps justifiable, but less honorable) don't creep in and inadvertently contaminate the message.

You need to clarify your intent so that you're not concerned about doing something that is not good in your own estimation. That way, you can proceed with confidence that this is what this person needs—even if they aren't going to like it—and that they can absolutely count on you to be there beside them, working through it with them.

Usually when you decide to confront someone it's because you understand that for the performer to improve, they need to be doing something differently; they need to stop, start or change something, and for some reason they can't seem to, or won't. You may not know why, but it has reached a point where, in your opinion, the change has to occur or there will be consequences that impact negatively on the task, on their relationship with colleagues, or with you or the company itself. Your job, as their coach, is to help them come up with a plan to resolve this impasse.

The purpose of this confrontation therefore is to come up with a plan to which both of you are committed and that will close the perceived gap while maintaining and building a relationship of respect and trust.

2. How do I want to present myself?

The reality is that you and the other person may see the world differently on this matter, and potentially powerful feelings (frustration, anger, embarrassment on your part; fear, anger, indignation on theirs) can get in the way of constructive discussion. So there's a lot at stake in terms of how you decide to present yourself.

If your image of yourself is of someone who is calm, decisive, friendly, fair and assertive, you need to be aware that this perception is about to be tested. Can you hold onto your self-identity—the kind of person you believe yourself to be—in the face of differences and powerful feelings, both yours and theirs? Well, yes, but to do so you need to prepare what you want to say and how you want to conduct yourself.

The ability to confront well does not come naturally. There's a tendency to think that if something feels uncomfortable or we aren't sure of the words, then we won't be any good at it. But the truth is, no one is naturally good at this. We need structure, we need a map, we need the skills and we need practice. That's what will make us feel competent and confident.

But I can tell you that if your intention is good and you hold yourself to your own standards of what constitutes good behavior, skill will not be as critical. That's why the first step is so important. Good intentions and self-management can carry the day even if your confronting skills aren't up to scratch. People sense when someone is on their side even if the words are being fumbled. Conversely, even the best-prepared speech will make no difference if your intentions don't match your words.

3. What, specifically, is the problem—the gap I want closed?

What is the core issue? Is it this person's impact on the team, chronic lateness, inability to listen, unwillingness to try the new program? Is it a relationship issue, a pattern you are seeing, or a specific behavior you want changed? What is causing the gap between your expectations and what is actually happening? Once you've determined the answer, you need to prepare a statement that clearly outlines the problem.

Then you need to formulate an accurate *description* of the most recent example—not your *interpretation* of what it means (the person is late, lazy, inconsiderate, rude), but a description stripped of personal feelings and reactions. To provide helpful feedback, you need to be able to separate facts and feelings. Keep your comments specific, describing the most recent example and focusing on the particular behavior.

If it's a simple, clearly defined problem such as the person not getting their expenses in on time, it's easy sailing. But often the problem is more complex, and it isn't easy to determine which of several potential issues you want to confront. If you latch on to the wrong problem, the solution will be wrong too.

If there are many issues within a single scenario, then you have to figure out which one you want to focus on in this confrontation. Often what looks like an issue is in fact a *consequence*. If you get the key issue right, other problems are easier to tackle. The ability to take an infraction to its bare essence takes patience, a sense of proportion (how much to bite off here) and precision.

In most cases what needs to change is not negotiable, in your mind, and what you are discussing together is how the change is going to occur. In some cases all you have is a clear description of a problem and the knowledge that there has to be a change, and together you and the performer must figure out what the change will be. In either case, it isn't enough to know what is bothering you; you must also be able to provide a clear description of the change you want and the problem you want to resolve. So what will help you with that?

Identify core issues. In analyzing a complex problem separate out core issues from consequences. While consequences are often the reason we need to confront, they are not what we want to focus on in our opening statement. Focus on a core behavior or action that needs to change. Many of the consequences will then drop away. Sometimes when we are unsure about whether to confront or not, a clear understanding of the consequences can help us decide. But they should never be the focus of your confrontation. Using consequences as the focus of your opening statement will inevitably lead you down paths that don't relate to the true problem at hand. So single out the core issue.

If the infraction has occurred once, it's a single event, and your feedback will be about *content*. If the same type of lapse occurs a second time, you may have to present it as a *pattern* that seems to be emerging. ("This is the second time this has occurred. You agreed it wouldn't happen again. I'm concerned that I can't count on you to keep your word.") Again, the message is clear: there is a history here, and history matters.

If the problem continues, talk about the *relationship*. This is far more significant than either content or pattern. Trust, competence and respect are all being called into question, and serious damage could occur, rendering a coaching relationship more difficult. ("Your inability to keep up your end of the agreement is putting me in the position of having to nag you to follow through. I'm not happy in that role. This is putting a major strain on our relationship. I don't feel I can trust you to keep your word.")

Decide what bothers you most. If there's a whole slew of possible problems, ask what you really want and don't want. Ask what you want for yourself, for the other person and for the relationship. In thinking about all three of these things you reduce the risk of letting one take a back seat and missing out on the most important problem. Bring some rigor to your analysis.

All of the suggestions above can help you analyze the problem, achieve clarity on why it is important and must be resolved, and narrow it down to the most important issue on which to focus.

Consider their story. Finally, in your analysis of the problem, consider their story. Ask yourself: What were the intentions of this person? Often we assume bad intentions because of the impact the person's behavior has had on others or on us. But their intentions may have been good, though misguided or inappropriate. You may not be able to find this out until you are interacting with the person. But do consider what intentions they may have had other than what you are attributing to them. Most people are driven by good intentions. If you really believe their intentions were negative, however, you may want to confront that rather than the behavior.

It's All about Me!

As you get further into your preparation you begin to see that **at least two-thirds of confrontation is about preparing and managing yourself** and one-third is about the other person. This is what tackling a challenging conversation is really all about. If I had to give this course another name it would be "It's all about me."

Our tendency is to think it's all about the other person. This can lead to lack of clarity on your part and inadequate planning ahead of time. When heading into a potentially difficult conversation, where there's likely to be a strong reaction, advance planning and preparation only make good sense. Being prepared helps you avoid the pitfall of finding you can't manage your own reactions, which can cause you to digress from a path that will help you achieve your goals as a coach.

The fact is, **it is usually your own self who gets in the way of your success, not the other person**. That's why you need the clarity, the skills and the map. They are what keep you on course in the heat of the moment. Having a map and knowing how to use the communication skills are big confidence-boosters—and building your own confidence is a big part of preparing.

It's usually at the emotional and verbal levels where problems seem to arise. When you're feeling pressured emotionally, there's a danger of just blurting out whatever words pop into your head when you're in the situation—and that simply won't do. You have to think carefully ahead of time about what you're going to say, and speak in a disciplined manner. You also have to have a plan for how to manage the difficult feelings you're bound to experience. This is a legitimate concern, because strong feelings can result in behavior you don't like in yourself.

There are two big risks here. One is that you might not live up to who you think you are; the other is that you may get results but damage the relationship. So let's move on to Step Two and look in more detail at the skills you'll need to communicate effectively and manage yourself with dignity and restraint.

Step Two: Prepare and Deliver the Opening Statement

The opening statement is absolutely critical for setting the tone of the rest of the interaction, so take the time to prepare it carefully and practice delivering it. You need to remember that despite your best intentions, you may have habits, words and behaviors that could sabotage that opening statement. It's perfectly normal to feel some tension at this time, and that's just when a distraction can throw you off course. This is definitely not a time to wing it!

"If you need to confront someone's behavior, do *not* begin by asking that person how things are going or by complimenting him or her," advises communications expert Susan Scott in her book *Fierce Conversations*.

"Don't surround your message with pillows. Come straight to the point. Say what you have to say in 60 seconds, then immediately extend an invitation to the other person to join the conversation."

Okay, now you know what *not* to say when creating your opening. Let's take a closer look at how to craft the opening.

Since the first few minutes of a difficult conversation are crucial to a successful outcome, you'll need to:

- Do your homework.
- Write it down.
- Practice saying it. Out loud.
- Time it, and get it down to 60 seconds.

In the literature on communication, there are many versions of how to conduct a confrontation. However, there is virtual unanimity on how to open such a conversation. When the problem is complicated and emotionally charged, thinking through your opening in the following way gives you your best shot at success.

Identify the core issue, then describe a specific and recent example. If you fail to identify the core issue, you risk losing focus and clarity during the remainder of the conversation. Select a specific example that illustrates the behavior or situation you want to change—the gap. Describe it. ("We need to talk about the timing for sending out your reports for our executive meetings. You sent your last report at 10 p.m. the night before our last meeting. I didn't have time to read and adequately analyze the content before the meeting the next morning. It is essential that everyone on the executive team has a chance to digest these numbers before the meeting. They have an impact on every decision we make.")

Describe your feelings about this issue. Telling someone how the situation affected you lets the person know that you have a vested interest in the change you want. ("I was irritated by the short amount of time you allowed us to analyze the information relative to our own areas.")

In describing feelings, which are always an important and difficult aspect of confrontation, people often mistakenly call something a feeling that is in fact a judgment or interpretation *colored* by feelings. ("I feel that you are dismissing me.") Dismissing is an action, not a feeling. How do you feel when someone dismisses you? Angry? Irritated? Unimportant? Susan Scott points out that if you can put the word *that* after the word *feeling*, you aren't describing a feeling.

Clarify the impact of this behavior. It's important to state clearly and calmly the effect the behavior will have. ("This is what is at stake—for me, for our department, for you . . .")

Identify your contribution to the problem. Ask yourself: How have I contributed to this situation? What has been my part in it? ("I may not have spelled out for you before how serious I believe the consequences for the team could be if we do not have adequate time to read and digest your numbers.") No long confession. You have 60 seconds for your entire opening statement.

Indicate your wish to resolve and invite the person to respond. Use the word *resolve*. ("I want to resolve this by the next meeting. Please tell me what was going on for you.") If you have created an atmosphere of safety, the other person will be open to the invitation to join the conversation.

Step Three: Explore Reality

The purpose of step three is to **drop your agenda and explore the other person's reality** through discussion to get a full understanding of the issue from their point of view.

All the skills in this step are designed to facilitate the process of gaining a better understanding of the issue so that you now hold both perspectives, not just yours. This process involves two skills I've already talked a great deal about: listening and asking questions. These skills actively communicate respect, which is important to the person you're confronting if they're to believe you are interested in moving forward *together*.

They also allow you to gain a deeper understanding of their perception and motivation.

Initially, most of us want the other person to change without considering how difficult or desirable it will be for them to do so. For joint problem-solving to take place, you need to consider what is realistic and what reciprocal change might be necessary. You can't do this without hearing the other person's point of view, and that's something many people are reluctant to do. You need effective tools to help you with this, especially if you aren't naturally so inclined.

The biggest obstacle to dropping your own agenda and listening to the other person effectively is usually an inability to manage resistance and reactions—on both sides. You want them to change, but people almost always resist change—some in small ways, by making excuses, and some in large ways, by growing angry and defensive. But you are also going to experience some resistance in yourself, particularly if you think you're right. If you're like most people, you are not going to want to change your well-thought-out perception, so you won't be open to hearing another version of events that might mean you have to do just that. You probably don't like the idea of changing your ideas about something you've been so sure of, so you'll resist. Your resistance may show up as impatience, dismissiveness, anger or indignation. To avoid these traps, you need to be prepared for your emotional responses in such situations and learn how to keep them contained. Managing resistance is an integral part of confronting. That's why this step requires self-discipline and on-the-spot self-management.

Let's take a closer look at the skills that will help you navigate this step successfully.

Explore the other person's reality. The only way to gain an understanding of the other person's reality is to get them talking and keep them talking. Asking open-ended questions to clarify the issues (probing for details and examples, floating a guess if they're finding it hard to verbalize, getting them to elaborate if their meaning isn't clear), listening attentively, paraphrasing where appropriate, and watching for non-verbal clues are activities that create a safe environment in which people will respond with more information. We cover asking effective questions and active listening in Chapter 2: Communication.

If you are going to understand this person's thinking, motivations and intentions as well as their blocks, you need to set aside your own interpretation of why they did something and what this means to you about the kind of person they are (lazy, rude, etc.). Most important, you need to find out what will enable or motivate them to move to the next step. It's not necessary to know what to say at this stage, but you do need to know how to communicate.

Getting them talking and keeping them talking, in what can be a tense or intimidating circumstance, can be challenging for a number of reasons. Which brings us to the second set of skills.

Manage reactions. They may not like what you have to say. In fact, they probably won't. You have to expect resistance. Whenever you're asking someone to change, you're bound to get some kind of pushback. It's natural, it's often justified, and it's definitely part of the process of change. *So assume that there will be resistance in some form and be prepared to handle it in a reasoned, exploratory way.* How you present the need for change—your opening—and how you manage the initial resistance will largely determine how severe and persistent the resistance is likely to be.

When the other person starts speaking, you may not like what they have to say or how they say it. You may be surprised by their perspective; you may disagree with it; you may be flabbergasted by it. If you're not prepared for this possibility, it can throw you off course and render you unable to listen and dig for full understanding. This can have one of two results, depending on the power structure: it will either shut them down or escalate the hostility.

It's hard to be open and curious about what they have to say when you're convinced you're right and you just wish they would "get it." So you may have a reaction in having to listen to a person who has, in your view, clearly got it all wrong.

What skills will you employ so that you don't overreact with indignation, frustration and blaming?

- Stick to the map and use the communication skills.
- Slow the conversation down; enlist silence.
- Reframe: step back and articulate the opportunities in the discussion.
- Stay the course and breathe!

Use silence. When people are feeling reactive—nervous, angry, threatened—it is quite common that the pace of a conversation picks up and lots of words start to fill the air with noise. This can become a self-fueling exchange, like a fire on which kindling continues to be thrown. When this occurs, it becomes difficult, if not impossible, to hear the other person's story or to connect with your own wisdom amid this noise, leaving no time for thoughtful consideration of what was just said and how to move the conversation forward. Yet it is at times like this that you most need to take the time to focus on what is truly important.

You have a much better chance of connecting with the true issue if the conversation progresses at a slower pace and there are spaces in which you can both reflect on what matters most.

Often, when you create some space—some moments of silence—the reactivity subsides and strong feelings lose their importance. It is during these moments that what really matters has a chance to emerge. Do not be afraid to make a request that calls for some silence or a slower pace. It can make a big difference to the outcome.

This means, of course, that you will need to notice—while it is happening—that the pace is too fast and there is too much "static." Susan

Scott, in *Fierce Conversations,* provides a useful list of the "signs that indicate silence is needed." Make a note of these cues that alert you to the need for silence and read them before going into a challenging conversation. They are a great aid in helping you identify when you are letting the conversation get off track and in reminding you that you need to intervene and slow the conversation down. Here are the cues that the conversation may be getting out of control. You are:

- talking over the person
- formulating your own response while the other person is talking
- responding quickly with little or no thought because you have to look clever, impressive and quick on your feet
- jumping in with advice before you have explored the other person's reality
- using silence or a break in the conversation to change the topic
- talking in circles, with nothing new emerging
- monopolizing the air time

Review and reframe. When emotions are running high, it's time to step back from the conversation and examine your focus. Is it what you intended to focus on? To get back on track it's also helpful to remind yourself of what opportunities there are in having this conversation.

Stay the course. Sometimes the conversation will take a turn you didn't expect. You discover that you have made a mistake or that your information has holes in it. The person may become upset with you as a result. Hang in there. Do not exit. If you started it, stay to the finish. There may be times when you just need to graciously say, "I was wrong. I made a mistake."

What is the other person likely to learn from this confrontation? If their behavior is a problem in the situation under discussion, it's sometimes a problem in other parts of their work and life. Letting them off the hook by not requiring them to self-reflect results in a lost opportunity to help them grow and get better at their job—which, as a coach with a developmental bias, is *your* job.

What are you learning as a coach? You may discover that you need to change something in yourself or in the environment. You need to be open to this, and recognize if you're resisting that change. This can often be your biggest block. ("I don't want to hear what *my* part is in this. I don't want to hear that *I* may have to do something different.")

Your number-one task here is to continue to create a safe environment for communication and ultimate resolution, even knowing that emotions are going to heat up. The more you're able to stick to the skills described here, the better you'll be able to manage yourself, manage the other person's resistance, promote mutual learning and come up with an effective plan to resolve an issue.

In terms of managing yourself, the most important thing to remember is to hold your purpose and task in mind and stick to the map. Predicting and planning how you are going to respond is far more helpful than trying to anticipate how *they* might respond.

- Stick to the map and use the skills.
- Practice active awareness in the moment; use listening skills.
- Know and recognize your triggers.
- Manage high arousal with a plan.
- Read Chapter 3.

Summarize. Now is the time to articulate what you have learned. You have told your story. You have fully explored their story. Now you are going to describe, without judgment, the gap between the two. You need to summarize what you've learned and confirm that the other person is on the same wavelength regarding what has to be resolved (never either/or, always both/and, as in "I need you to be here on time and you say you can't because of your child-care situation").

Once you have summarized the situation, check with the other person to confirm that they're in agreement and to make sure that the two of you have the same understanding of what needs to be resolved. ("Does that sound like an accurate summary of where we are? Is there anything else that needs to be said?")

Step Four: Resolve and Plan

The purpose of Step Four is to create an action plan together and set up accountability. You work with your partner to resolve the problem by:

- exploring options
- choosing one and agreeing on how to move forward
- checking for commitment
- planning for ongoing communication and accountability

It is very important at this stage to continue asking questions, thereby allowing your partner to create the bulk of the plan. By asking, "How do we move forward from here?" you're encouraging the other person's participation in working toward a solution. This is an opportunity for them to take ownership of and responsibility for the specifics.

Both parties must create the plan, and both parties must have something to do when the talking is done.

A plan for ongoing communication and accountability needs to be established at this time as well. Offer your support. Set up times for checking in with each other and the best means for doing so.

Finally, check for commitment. Ask: "Do you see this agreement as a positive step?" "Can you see yourself following through on this agreement?"

Extinguishers have no plan.

- They don't prepare themselves and have no clear purpose other than "You've got to change."
- They "wing it," often getting the conversation off to a rocky start.
- They get defensive if there's any disagreement over their "facts."
- They dictate the solution to the other person or, if they are afraid of confrontation, never really get to any resolution because they chicken out.

To be an Igniter remember this!

- Prepare yourself. Clarify your purpose. Clarify how you want to present yourself. Analyze the problem and identify the gap.
- Prepare and deliver an opening statement.
- Develop a full understanding of the problem by exploring their reality.
- Create a plan together to resolve the problem.